# Vintage Alexander

By Florence Theriault • Gold Horse Publishing

To order additional copies, contact:

Dollmasters, P.O. Box 2319, Annapolis, MD 21401

Tel. 800-966-3655, Fax 410-571-9605

www.dollmasters.com

Research Assistance by Nelly Farge Theriault

Design by Deborah VanDereedt
Photography by Chris Brady and Colby Kuschatka

This book is based upon a collection of dolls auctioned by Theriault's of Annapolis, Maryland.

$39
ISBN: 1-931503-12-5
Printed in Hong Kong

# Foreword

In America, an object is officially an antique when it reaches the age of 100. In this book are a number of dolls are that are reaching that status, and yet, in the collecting world, the notion remains that the Alexander doll is merely modern, a term used with a slightly pejorative edge. It's time to change that, and time for collectors of antique dolls to cast a new look at these classic beauties.

If they're not yet exactly antiques, dolls by Alexander can certainly be labeled as vintage. And age has done well by them. Created with the highest standards of design and production, the dolls are imaginative and complete, in every respect. The firm's founder, Madame Alexander, brought from her European heritage a sense of propriety and good taste, and balanced this with American imagination and free spirit.

Always, she used the finest fabrics, the perfectly scaled accessories, and just the right accessories. There is an adage about fashion that if you look at a complete costume and one element "sticks out", then it is wrong. Each aspect of a costume should complement the other, none taking the foreground, none shadowing the others, yet nothing missing. That rule has always prevailed with the dolls of Madame Alexander, and the collector who views these dolls today will instantly recognize this.

When they first appear, fashionable dolls are models of current style. As the years go along they become valuable objects in our study of the past, miniature models of historical fashion. A study of the doll manufacturer's catalogs underlies this study, emphasizing what the maker considered new and exciting in the world of fashion, the colors, the fabrics, the accessories, the way to wear, and the place to wear the new styles. A study of the actual dolls and their costumes completes the experience adding the dimensional and posing qualities that no flat image could truly show.

Doll collectors and social historians have long understood the value of the antique doll and its wardrobe in viewing historic fashions. It is time they begin to value the Alexander doll in that light, too.

Florence Theriault
December, 2002

# Dolls Are Little People
### by
# Madame Alexander

### 1. Composition Bride with Blonde Hair

14" (35 cm). Composition socket-head, brown sleep eyes, real lashes, painted lower lashes, smoky eyeshadow, bow-shaped closed mouth, blonde mohair wig with original coiffure and soft curls, five-piece composition body. Excellent unplayed with condition with slightest faint lines on face and limbs, few wear holes in veil and spots on underskirt. MARKS: Mme Alexander (doll and costume). The bride wears original costume comprising embroidered tulle wedding gown with hooped taffeta underslip and bodice, panties, shoes and socks, pearl necklace, lilies of the valley on the long trained veil, bouquet of wedding flowers, and has original gold-paper label on her wrist. Circa 1940. $400/500

### 2. Composition Tiny Betty Bride and Bridesmaids

Each 7" (18 cm). Each doll has one piece composition head and torso, painted facial features with side-glancing eyes, tiny closed mouth, jointed arms and legs, painted shoes and socks. Excellent condition. MARKS: Mme. Alexander (dolls and costumes). The wedding party comprises brunette bride in embroidered tulle gown with veil, pearls, lilies of valley coronet and bouquet, hooped skirt and panties; auburn-haired bridesmaid with yellow gown with blue centered flowers, peach slip, flowered cap and bouquet; and blonde bridesmaid in matching lavender ensemble with fuschia-tinted flowers. Circa 1935. $650/900

### 3. Composition Tiny Betty Bride And Bridesmaid

Each 7" (18 cm). Each doll has one-piece composition head and torso, painted facial features with side-glancing eyes, tiny closed mouth, jointed arms and legs, painted shoes and socks. Good condition, nose tip of bride chipped. MARKS: Mme. Alexander (dolls and costumes). The bride wears original embroidered tulle gown and veil, hooped underskirt, pantalets. The bridesmaid wears (faded) blue organdy gown with pink trim and underskirt, panties, ruffled lace cap. Circa 1935. $200/250 (not illustrated)

### 4. Composition Bride with Embroidered Tulle Gown

21" (53 cm). Composition socket-head, dark blue sleep eyes, real lashes, painted lower lashes, smoky eyeshadow, bow-shaped closed mouth, original blonde human hair in original coiffure with ringlet curls onto the shoulders and cascade of smaller curls at the back of head, five-piece composition body. Excellent condition, few very faint surface lines on face. MARKS: Madame Alexander (costume). The bride wears original costume comprising embroidered tulle wedding gown with hooped taffeta underskirt and panties, shoes, socks, lace-edged veil with coronet of lilies of the valley, and carrying matching floral bouquet, original gold-paper tag "Created by Madame Alexander" on wrist. Circa 1940. $700/900

### 5. Composition Bridesmaid In Rose Gown

18" (46 cm). Composition socket-head, blue sleep eyes, real lashes, painted lower lashes, smoky eyeshadow, bow-shaped closed mouth, light brown mohair wig with original coiffure and soft curls, five-piece composition body. Excellent condition, paint flake on left elbow, tiny holes in dress. Marks: Mme. Alexander (doll and costume). The bridesmaid wears original costume comprising rose sheer-nylon gown with rose nylon satin trim, matching petticoat and panties, nylon muff with flowers and a matching coronet of flowers in her hair. Circa 1940. $400/500

### 6. Composition Portrait Lady "Orchard Princess" in Lavender Gown

21"(53 cm). Composition socket-head with heart-shaped face, large brown sleep eyes, real lashes, three painted long lashes at outside corner of each eye, blue eyeshadow, dark eyeliner, brushstroked brows, closed O-shaped mouth, brunette hair in elaborate coiffure with cascading beads at the back, five-piece composition body with adult female shape. Excellent condition, Marks: Madame Alexander New York (undergarment tag). The portrait lady wears her original lavender nylon brocade gown with padded bosom, purple velvet banner with flowers, elbow-length ball gloves, turqoise beaded bracelet, star earrings, petticoat, pantalets, purple slippers. 1946, made for one year only. $1800/2200

## 7. Four Composition Tiny Betty Dolls As "Little Women" in Original Boxes

each 7" (18 cm). Each doll has one piece composition head and torso, painted facial features with side-glancing eyes, tiny closed mouth, mohair wig in blonde or brunette, jointed arms and legs, painted shoes and stockings. Excellent condition. MARKS: Mme. Alexander (dolls and costumes, each costume also labeled with name of doll). Each doll wears her original costume in vibrant cotton colors, with undergarments. Each doll is preserved in its original flowered yellow box with name of doll. Circa 1935. $1500/2000

## 8. Composition Tiny Betty in Swedish Costume

7" (18 cm). One-piece composition head and torso, painted facial features with side-glancing eyes, tiny closed mouth, blonde mohair wig, jointed arms and legs with painted shoes. Excellent condition. MARKS: Mme. Alexander (doll and costume, costume also tagged "Swedish"). Original costume of muslin blouse and bonnet, yellow cotton skirt over stiffened petticoat and pantalets, red felt vest, striped cotton apron. Circa 1935. $300/400

## 9. Composition Tiny Betty as Polish Girl

7" (18 cm). One-piece composition head and torso, painted facial features, side-glancing eyes, tiny closed mouth, blonde mohair curly wig, jointed composition arms and legs with painted shoes and socks. Excellent condition. MARKS: Mme. Alexander (doll) Polish, Madame Alexander (costume). The doll wears her original white organdy dress with tri-color rayon ribbon banding, green felt vest, flowers in hair. Circa 1935. $300/400

## 10. Composition Tiny Betty as "Birthday Girl"

7" (18 cm). One-piece composition head and torso, painted facial features with side-glancing eyes, tiny closed mouth, brunette mohair wig, jointed arms and legs, painted shoes and socks. Good condition, light facial crazing, composition split inside upper left leg, some costume staining. MARKS: Mme Alexander (doll and costume, also "Birthday Girl" on

costume). Original costume comprising blue cotton dress with red rick-rack trim, stiffened yellow muslin cape with red lined hood, petticoat, pantalets. Circa 1935. $200/300

### 11. Composition Tiny Betty as "Carmen Miranda"
7" (18 cm). One-piece composition head and torso, painted facial features with side-glancing eyes, tiny closed mouth, black mohair wig, jointed arms and legs, painted shoes and socks. Excellent condition. MARKS: Mme. Alexander (on doll and costume). Original costume portraying Carmen Miranda comprises ivory satin skirt with pink and green rick-rack trim, green bead trimmed halter, colorful beads, fruit and flower trimmed feather cap, stiffened petticoat, pantalets. Circa 1939. $500/700

### 12. Composition Little Betty as "Peasant"
9" (23 cm). Composition socket-head, painted facial features, side-glancing eyes, jointed composition arms and legs, brunette mohair wig. Excellent condition. MARKS: Wendy Ann, Mme. Alexander, New York (doll) "Peasant" by Madame Alexander (costume). The doll wears original gown with flowered bodice, green cotton skirt, attached striped apron, green bandana, pantalets, shoes and socks. Circa 1935. $300/400

### 13. Composition Little Betty as Japanese Girl
9" (23 cm). Composition socket-head, painted facial features, blue side-glancing eyes, jointed composition arms and legs, black mohair wig. Excellent condition, wig a bit sparse. MARKS: Wendy Ann Mme. Alexander (doll and costume). The doll wears original patterned tunic, green cotton pants, shoes, socks, red sash, and a coronet of daisies in her hair. Circa 1935. $300/400

### 14. Composition Little Betty as Hawaiian Girl
9" (23 cm). Brown-complexioned composition socket-head, brown side-glancing eyes, jointed composition arms and legs. Excellent condition. MARKS: Mme. Alexander (doll), Hawaiian (costume tag). The doll wears original costume including "grass" skirt, necklace, red sandals. Circa 1939. $500/600

### 15. Composition Little Betty
9" (23 cm). Composition socket-head, blue side-glancing eyes, brunette mohair wig, jointed composition arms and legs. Good condition. MARKS: Wendy Ann Mme. Alexander (doll), Madame Alexander (costume). The doll wears original costume comprising vividly printed cotton skirt, overblouse, red bandana, pantalets, red boots. Circa 1939. $300/400

### 16. Pair, Composition Little Betty Dolls As Spanish Boy and Girl
9" (23 cm). Each has composition socket-head, painted facial features, brown side-glancing eyes, black mohair wig, jointed composition arms and legs. Excellent condition, girl has tiny split at throat. MARKS: Mme Alexander (dolls and costumes, costumes also labeled "Spanish"). The boy and girl wear original costumes, he with black felt pants, red shirt, straw hat with red pom-poms, black shoes, socks; she with white organdy blouse attached to red cotton skirt with yellow and green rayon ribbons, black lace mantilla, chemise, shoes and socks. Circa 1939. $400/500

### 17. Trio, Composition Little Betty Dolls

9" (23 cm). Each has composition socket-head, painted blue side-glancing eyes, black or blonde mohair wig, jointed composition arms and legs. Excellent condition, some light craze lines. MARKS: Mme. Alexander (three dolls and three costumes). Included is Carmen Mirand and Dutch Boy, each in well detailed original costume. Circa 1939. $600/800

### 18. Pair, Composition Tiny Betty Dolls

7" (18 cm). Each has one-piece composition head and torso, painted facial features, blue side-glancing eyes, blonde mohair wig, jointed composition arms and legs with painted shoes and socks. Excellent condition, except craze lines on face of Belgian girl. MARKS: Mme Alexander (dolls). Belgian Madame Alexander (blue dressed girl) (costume of yellow dressed girl is unmarked). The dolls each wear their original factory costumes. Circa 1939. $300/500

### 19. Composition Little Betty as "McGuffey Ana"

9" (23 cm). Composition socket-head, painted facial features, blue side-glancing eyes, tiny closed mouth, blonde human hair braids, jointed arms and legs. Excellen condition. MARKS: Mme. Alexander (torso) "McGuffey Ana" Madame Alexander (costume). The doll wears her original pink and white checkered dress, organdy pinafore, straw bonnet, bloomers, shoes, socks, and has original gold-paper label "Created by Madame Alexander". Circa 1939. $300/400

### 20. Two, Composition Tiny Betty Dolls As David Copperfield and Alice in Wonderland

7" (18 cm). Each has one piece composition head and torso, painted facial features, side-glancing blue eyes, tiny closed mouth, blonde or light brown mohair wig, jointec arms and legs with painted shoes and socks. Excellent condition, slight craze line above his lip. MARKS: Mme. Alexander (dolls) Charles Dickens "David Copperfield" (costume tag on boy). Each doll wears original factory costume, he with striped pant: wide collar shirt with bow-tie, black felt jacket and hat; she with mauve taffeta dress with rick-rack trim, organdy apron and collar, slip, panties. Circa 1935. $400/500

### 21. Composition "McGuffey Ana" in Original Box

13" (33 cm). Composition socket-head, blue sleep eyes, real lashes, painted lower lashes, feathered brows, open mouth, blonde human hair in long braids with curly bangs, five-piece composition body. Excellent condition. MARKS: 13 (torso) "McGuffey Ana" Madame Alexander (cloth tag). The doll wears her original blue organdy dress, pink patterned pinafore with ruffled bretelles, cotton slip with attached panties, white socks, black ankle boots, straw bonnet with flowers, and is contained in original box labeled McGuffey Ana, model #1228. Circa 1938. $800/1000

### 22. Composition "Flora McFlimsey" in Original Box

15" (38 cm). Composition socket-head, brown sleep eyes, real lashes, painted lower lashes, freckles across the nose, open mouth, four teeth, brunette human hair in original factory coiffure with braids and curls, five-piece composition body. Excellent condition. MARKS: Princess Elizabeth Alexander Doll Co. (doll) "Flora McFlimsey of Madison Square" by Madame Alexander (costume). The doll wears original peach cotton dress with blue and striped ribbon bands, attached pantalets, stockings, ankle boots, peach ribbons in hair, has original gold-paper wrist tag, and original box with green and purple label stamped Flora McFlimsey, model #2302. Circa 1938. $800/1000

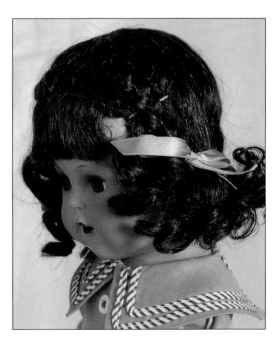

**23. Composition Child "Kate Greenaway"**
13" (33 cm). Composition socket-head, brown sleep eyes, real lashes, painted lower lashes, open mouth, four teeth, blonde mohair wig, five-piece composition body. Good condition, some craze lines on face, split by right eye. MARKS: 13 (torso) Kate Greenaway Madame Alexander (costume tag). The doll wears her original costume of cream cotton with floral patterned borders at bodice and hem, and on sleeves and matching purse, orange taffeta bonnet, black lace fingerless gloves, slip, panties with red ribbon lacing, black strap shoes, socks. Circa 1940. $500/700

**24. Composition "Fairy Princess"**
15" (38 cm). Composition socket-head, blue sleep eyes, real lashes, painted lower lashes, smoky eyeshadow, feathered brows, bow-shaped ruby lips, strawberry-blonde mohair wig in long curls, five-piece composition body. Excellent condition, slight surface flaking on limbs, few torso craze lines. MARKS: Mme. Alexander (head). "Sleeping Beauty" Madame Alexander (costume). The doll wears her original burnt-orange taffeta gown with gold

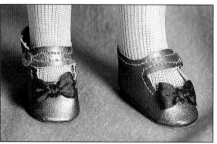

metallic trim, matching tiara, petticoat, pants, stockings, gold shoes with orange bows. 1938. $800/1000

## 25. Composition "Princess Elizabeth" with Original Box

17" (43 cm). Composition socket-head, green sleep eyes, real lashes, painted lower lashes, open mouth, teeth, blonde human hair in original arranged coiffure, five-piece composition body. Excellent condition, eyes faded. MARKS: Princess Elizabeth Madame Alexander (doll and costume). The doll wears her original magenta taffeta gown with lace trim, cream velvet cape with ermine trim, petticoat, pants, gold shoes and socks, metallic headband. The doll has her

original Princess Elizabeth hang tag with illustration of the doll, and original box with gold label having photograph of the doll, identified as model #3984M. Circa 1937. $800/1200

## 26. Composition "Princess Elizabeth" With Tiara

13" (33 cm). Composition socket-head, blue sleep eyes, real lashes, painted lower lashes, open mouth, four teeth, blonde mohair wig, five-piece composition body. Very good condition, light surface lines, repair to small split at back neck socket. MARKS: 13 (doll), Princess Elizabeth Madame Alexander (costume). The doll wears original blue (lavender) gown with blue lace sleevelets and trim, petticoat, pants, shoes and socks, and has "jeweled" tiara with crown symbol. Circa 1937. $400/500

**27. Set, American Composition Dionne Quintuplet Toddlers**

8" (20 cm). Each has composition socket-head with painted short brown hair, painted brown side-glancing eyes, bow-shaped mouth, five-piece composition toddler body. Excellent condition. MARKS: Alexander (dolls). The dolls wear original factory costumes, comprising pastel organdy dresses with rick-rack trim, matching petticoats with ribbon trim, pants, matching bonnets, shoes, socks, each with original Dionne Quintuplet name tag. Circa 1936. $1100/1400

**28. Six Composition Toddlers**
**From Exhibition at 1939 World's Fair**

12" (30 cm). Each has composition socket-head, sleep eyes, real lashes, painted lower lashes, open mouth, five-piece toddler body. The five boy dolls have side-parted human hair; the girl has blonde mohair curly wig. Good condition overall, eyes faded, some retouch on facial complexion. MARKS: Madame Alexander (dolls and costumes). The five boys wear romper suits with white dotted Swiss attached skirts (three yellow, one green, one pink), shoes and socks. The girl wears blue dotted Swiss dress with pale blue rayon sash, long slip, shoes and socks. The rare dolls were commissioned from the Alexander firm to be shown at a University of California exhibition "Demonstration of Human Heredity" at the Hall of Science in the 1939 World's Fair. (Articles documenting the history of the dolls are included.) Circa 1939. $1200/1500

**29. Composition "Nurse Betty" for Dionne Quintuplets**

13" (33 cm). Composition socket-head, brown sleep eyes, real lashes, painted lower lashes, closed mouth, blonde mohair wig, five-piece composition body. Excellent condition. MARKS: Madame Alexander New York (costume). The doll, representing Nurse Betty from Dionne Quintuplets fame, wears her original white cotton nurse's uniform and cap, slip, panties, shoes and socks. Circa 1936. $700/900

**30. Composition "Doctor Dafoe" for Dionne Quintuplets**

14" (35 cm). Composition socket-head with painted facial features, pale blue eyes, closed mouth with wide smile, deep cheek dimples, grey mohair wig, five-piece composition body. Excellent condition, missing spectacles. MARKS: Madame Alexander New York (costume). The doll, portraying Doctor Dafoe of Dionne Quintuplets fame, wears his original cotton doctor's uniform with tunic, shoes, socks. The face was uniquely modeled for this doll. Circa 1936. $900/1200

**31. Composition Wendy-Ann in Riding Costume**

13" (33 cm). Composition socket-head, brown sleep eyes, real lashes, painted lower lashes, smoky eyeshadow, bow-shaped closed mouth, blonde human hair, six-piece composition body with swivel waist. Excellent condition. MARKS: Wendy-Ann Alexander New York (doll). The doll wears her factory original costume comprising white blouse, red vest with brass buttons, black tie, yellow gabardine twill riding pants, navy blue felt cloche, shoes, socks. Circa 1936. $400/500

### 32. Composition "Jane Withers" in Yellow Dress

13" (33 cm). Composition socket-head, green sleep eyes, real lashes, painted lower lashes, closed mouth with slightly smiling expression, brunette mohair curly wig, five-piece composition body. Excellent condition. MARKS: Madame Alexander New York USA (costume). The doll wears original costume comprising dress with dotted Swiss bodice and yellow cotton skirt with attached petticoat, panties, matching bonnet, black velvet trims, socks, black strap shoes. Circa 1937. $800/1100

### 33. Composition "Sonja Henie" in Yellow Skating Costume

15" (38 cm). Composition socket-head, brown sleep eyes, real lashes, painted lower lashes, smoky eyeshadow, open mouth with smiling expression, teeth, dimples, blonde mohair wig in original factory coiffure, five-piece composition body. Excellent condition. MARKS: Alexander Sonja Henie (head), Genuine "Sonja Henie" Madame Alexander (costume). The doll wears her original yellow taffeta skating costume with green net petticoat and taffeta panties, skates, green taffeta bow in hair, and has original paper hang tag with photograph of the skating celebrity. Circa 1940. $800/1000

### 33A. Composition "Sonja Henie" in Ski Costume

15" (38 cm). Composition socket-head, brown sleep eyes, real lashes, painted lower lashes, smoky eyeshadow, open mouth, four teeth, dimpled cheeks, blonde mohair wig in original factory coiffure, five-piece composition body. Excellent condition. MARKS: Genuine "Sonja Henie" Madame Alexander USA (costume). The doll wears original ski costume comprising red jacket, blue pants, panties, socks, shoes, flowers in hair, along with wooden skis and wooden ski pole. Circa 1942. $800/1000

### 34. Composition "Sonja Henie"
### In Ivory Skating Costume, in Original Box

13" (33 cm). Composition socket-head, brown sleep eyes, real lashes, painted lower lashes, smoky eyeshadow, open mouth with wide smile, four teeth, dimpled cheeks, blonde human hair in original factory coiffure, six-piece Wendy Ann composition body with swivel waist. Excellent condition. MARKS: Wendy-Ann Mme. Alexander New York (doll), Genuine "Sonja Henie" Doll Madame Alexander (costume). The doll wears original ivory satin skating costume with faux-fur trim, stiffened net petticoat, ivory satin panties, skates, fabric roses trim the waistband and her hair. The doll is presented in her original Alexander box with photograph of the celebrity skater, identified as model #1400E. Circa 1940. $900/1300

### 35. Composition "Sonja Henie"
### In Pink Taffeta Skating Costume

20" (51 cm). Composition socket-head, brown sleep eyes, real lashes, painted lower lashes, smoky eyeshadow, open mouth, four teeth, blonde human hair in original factory curls, five-piece composition body. Excellent condition, slightest surface line, unplayed with. MARKS: Genuine "Sonja Henie" by Madame Alexander (costume tag). The doll wears her original pink taffeta skating ensemble with faux-fur skirt trim, petticoat, taffeta panties, gold skates. Circa 1940. $800/1100

### 36. Composition "Soldier" in WWII Uniform

15" (38 cm). Composition socket-head, blue sleep eyes, real lashes, painted lower lashes, smoky eyeshadow, bow-shaped closed mouth, blonde mohair wig, five-piece composition body. Excellent condition. MARKS: Mme. Alexander (doll and costume). The doll wears original soldier's uniform of WWII, comprising brown cotton-twill jacket and trousers, brass buttons, leather-like belt, green khaki jacket and tie, brown soldier's hat with leatherlike brim and brass buttons. Circa 1943. $600/800

### 37. Composition W.A.A.C. in WWII Uniform

15" (38 cm). Composition socket-head, brown sleep eyes, real lashes, painted lower lashes, smoky eyeshadow, bow-shaped closed mouth, auburn mohair wig, five-piece composition body. Excellent condition. MARKS: Mme. Alexander (doll) W.A.A.C. Madame Alexander (costume). The doll wears original light brown cotton twill uniform with belted jacket, flared skirt, green khaki shirt and tie, light brown cap with eagle emblem, shoes, socks, and carries brown portfolio and gloves. Circa 1943. $600/800

### 38. Composition W.A.V.E. in WWII Uniform

15" (38 cm). Composition socket-head, brown sleep eyes, real lashes, painted lower lashes, smoky eyeshadow, bow-shaped closed mouth, brunette mohair wig, five-piece composition body. Excellent condition. MARKS: Mme. Alexander (doll), W.A.V.E. Madame Alexander (costume). The doll wears original navy blue cotton uniform with brass buttons, blue and white cap with eagle trim, shoes and socks, slip and panties, and carries portfolio and gloves. Circa 1943. $600/800

### 39. Set, Composition "Snow White, Seven Dwarves, and Wicked Stepmother" Marionettes

9"–12" (23–30 cm). Each has composition head with painted facial features to portray the various storybook figures, with sculpted hair or hat, distinctive features such as beards, hair ribbons, or witch's wart. Each puppet has composition torso, hands and feet, and loosely-jointed limbs to allow puppet articulation. Excellent condition with some minor light crazing. MARKS: Madame Alexander New York (costumes, with name of each figure). Each of the Dwarves, Snow White and Wicked Stepmother wear original Alexander factory costumes, with

original puppet strings and wooden handles. Included is one box with original label "Walt Disney's Marionettes, Alexander Doll Co." The marionettes were designed by Tony Sarg for Alexander, circa 1940. $800/1200

**40. Composition "Donald Duck" Marionette**
9" (23 cm). Composition head portraying the comic character Donald Duck with painted features and beak, composition body, hands and orange webbed feet, loosely articulated limbs and head that operate from puppet string and wooden handle. Very good condition, slight paint wear on the beak. MARKS: Walt Disney's Marionette "Donald Duck" Madame Alexander (costume tag). The duck wears original red cotton marching jacket and black faux-fur hat. Circa 1940. $400/500

**41. Composition Pig in Blue Overalls**
11" (28 cm). Composition socket-head portraying a cheerful-faced pig, painted facial features, down-glancing eyes, snout, five-piece composition toddler body. Excellent condition. MARKS: Madame Alexander (doll and costume). The pig wears his original blue overalls, white felt gloves and white cap. Circa 1940. $400/500

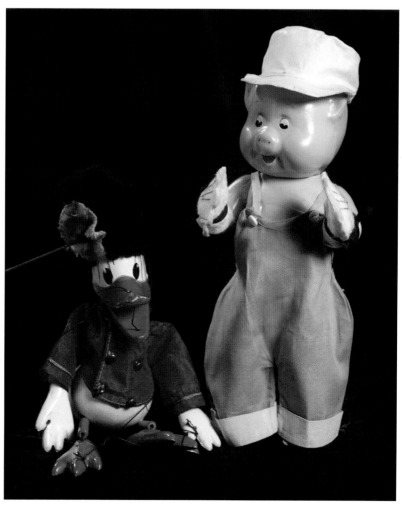

### 42. Cloth "Alice in Wonderland" with Yarn Hair
21" (53 cm). Flat-dimensional cloth doll with printed facial features, wide-open side-glancing eyes, O-shaped mouth, blonde yarn hair, stitch-jointed body with separate thumbs. Good condition, some slight spotting. MARKS: Original Alice in Wonderland (costume tag). The doll wears her original gingham printed orange/cream dress with attached panties, organdy apron and collar, shoes and socks. Circa 1940. $400/500

### 43. Cloth "Posey Pet" with Striped Dress
17" (43 cm). Brown plush cat with pink-lined stitched ears, flower-shaped velvet eyes with black bead centers, black velvet petal-shaped nose, stitched limbs. Very good condition, some costume spotting. MARKS: "Posey Pet" (cloth tag). The animal-doll wears its original red and white striped cotton dress with attached blue cotton apron rick-rack trim, pantalets, felt bonnet with flower trim. Circa 1940. $600/800

### 44. Cloth "Posey Pet" with Organdy Dress in Original Box
17" (43 cm). White plush rabbit with pink-lined stitched-on ears has pink and purple felt-edged purple eyes, long eyelashes, heart-shaped mouth, cotton print stitch-jointed body with white plush paws. Excellent condition. MARKS: "Posey Pet" by Madame Alexander (original yellow tag on wrist), Madame Alexander (costume tag). The animal-doll wears original yellow organdy dress, matching pantalets, pink organdy apron, felt bonnet with green silk streamers, flower trim, with original paper tag and original box. Circa 1940. $900/1100

**45. Cloth "Bobby Q" and "Susie Q" in Original Boxes**
13" and 15" (33 and 38 cm). Mask-face dolls with pressed printed features depicting little school girl and boy, side-glancing large eyes, blushed cheeks, she with yellow yarn braids, he with auburn/brown curly hair, each with peach muslin stitch-jointed body, she with red and white stitched-on stockings, he with blue and white stitched-on stockings. Excellent condition. MARKS: "Susie Q" (or "Bobby Q"), Madame Alexander N.Y. (costumes and tags). She wears original green felt suit with magenta collar, buttons and trim, white felt spats, black felt shoes, red paper purse-shaped tag, straw bonnet with cherry and magenta trim; he with green felt jacket, plaid cotton trousers and bow-tie, straw bowler hat, white felt spats, black felt shoes, carrying paper "4th grade reader". Each is contained in its original box with illustration and stamped model numbers 9/3100 and 9/3101. Circa 1940. $1600/2200

**46. Pair, Cloth Bunny Belle and Beau Brummel**
13" (33 cm). Each with mask-face having pressed printed features, blue side-glancing eyes, green felt bunny ears with pink felt lining, rosy cheeks, tiny mouth, she with green polka dot cotton stuffed body, he with yellow polka-dot cotton stuffed body. Excellent condition. MARKS: Madame Alexander New York (cloth tags on costumes). She has fleecy curly yarn hair, wears original yellow organdy dress and pantalets with lace trim, green felt coat, striped taffeta bow, white felt spats, black felt shoes. He has short blonde pigtails, wears green felt long fitted coat over blue cotton trousers, black shoes with pom-poms, straw hat with feathered trim. Circa 1935. $1200/1800.

**47. Pair, Velvet and Yarn Black Poodles**
16" (40 cm). Each has firmly shaped black velvet body with shaped nose, stitched-on lavender lined ears, tufts of "fur" (actually curly black yarn) at top of head, nose, paws, ear tips, collar and tail, lavender and white felt eyeliner, large black bead eyes, heart-shaped mouth. Excellent condition. MARKS: Madame Alexander New York (cloth tag on each). He has brass monocle, white felt collar and bow-tie, lapel flower; she has magenta bow in hair, metallic trimmed magenta silk-like neck bow, lapel roses. Circa 1950. $600/900

**48. Velvet and Yarn Black Poodle**
16" (40 cm). Firmly shaped black velvet body with shaped nose, stitched-on lavender lined ears, tufts of "fur" at top of head, nose, paws, ear tips, collar and tail, lavender and grey felt eyeliner, black bead eyes with long curly eyelashes, heart-shaped mouth. Excellent condition. MARKS: Madame Alexander New York (cloth tag). She wears magenta taffeta hair and neck bows, little roses at lapel. Circa 1950. $400/500

### 49. Cloth "Little Shaver" in Original Box
11" (28 cm). Cloth mask-face with pressed and painted facial features, side glancing eyes, tiny button-shaped nose, tiny closed mouth, blonde floss hair, pink stockinette body. Near mint condition. MARKS: Little Shaver, Madame Alexander (cloth costume tag). The doll wears original gown with magenta taffeta blouse, blue nylon ruffled skirt and sleeves, black lace fingerless gloves, magenta purse, black velvet shoes, an arrangement of black lace and flowers in hair, and has original box labeled model #3800. Circa 1940. $500/700

### 50. Cloth "Little Shaver" by Alexander
20" (51 cm). Cloth mask-face with pressed and painted facial features, large round side-glancing eyes, painted upper lashes, tiny clothed mouth, brown fleece-yarn hair in marcelled curls, pink stockinette firmly stuffed body. Excellent condition. MARKS: "Little Shaver" Madame Alexander New York (cloth tag on costume). The doll wears original blue taffeta blouse with attached peach nylon skirt with attached pink cotton petticoat, matching panties, blue taffeta purse with little flowers, black lace fingerless gloves, a posy of flowers with black net at top of head, black velvet shoes. Circa 1940. $800/1000

### 51. Cloth "Little Shaver" in Smaller Size
9" (23 cm). Cloth mask-face with pressed and painted facial features, side-glancing eyes, painted upper lashes, O-shaped mouth, blonde floss hair, stockinette body. Excellent condition. MARKS: "Little Shaver" Madame Alexander (costume). The doll wears original gown having magenta taffeta bodice, blue nylon skirt with velvet magenta ribbon bands, taffeta purse, fingerless gloves, black velvet shoes, flowers and lace in hair. Circa 1940. $400/500

**52. Hard Plastic "Victoria"
From "Me and My Shadow Series"**
18" (46 cm). Hard plastic socket-head with
Maggie face, large blue sleep eyes, real lashes,
painted lower side lashes, umber eye shadow,
upturned nose, closed mouth, dark blonde wig in
original factory coiffure, five-piece hard plastic
walking style body. Excellent condition. MARKS:
Madame Alexander (costume). The doll wears
original costume described in the 1954
Alexander catalog as "reminiscent of 1850" with
"slate blue faille taffeta with side panniers and
bustle drapery delicately etched with narrow
white silk braids" and a "tiny hat of starched
white lace [with] topknot of roses and forget-me-
nots", with taffeta petticoat, pantalets, stockings,
black one-strap shoes, velvet reticule. Model
#2030C, "Victoria" from "Me and My Shadow"
series, 1954. $1100/1500

**53. Hard Plastic "Cherie"
From "Me and My Shadow" Series**
18" (46 cm). Hard plastic socket-head, large blue glass sleep eyes, real lashes, painted side lashes, closed mouth with bow-shaped red lips, dark blonde hair in original factory coiffure, five-piece hard plastic walking body. Near mint condition. MARKS: Madame Alexander (costume). The doll is "dressed for the opera" according to the 1954 Alexander catalog wearing "bouffant gown of heavy white satin caught up in a graceful drapery with bright pink roses. Her full length opera coat of Goya pink taffeta is lined and fastened at the throat with a dashing big bow", along with rosebud coronet, pink satin bag, taffeta hooped petticoat, panties, stockings, ivory satin shoes. Model #2030B, "Cherie" from "Me and My Shadow" series, 1954. $1200/1700

### 54. Hard Plastic "John Robert Powers" Model

15" (38 cm). Hard plastic socket-head with Maggie-model face, brown sleep eyes, real lashes, unusual painting of lower lashes, blonde hair in factory arrangement, five-piece hard plastic body. Excellent condition. MARKS: "John Powers Model" Madame Alexander (costume). The doll wears her original white organdy blouse, purple twirl skirt with charm-decorated cinch belt, pink petticoat and panties, white stockings, black strap shoes, red velvet beret, and carries hat box labeled "Madame Alexander presents the John Robert Powers Model" containing curlers and comb. The doll has her original gold wrist tag. Circa 1952. $1100/1400

### 55. Hard Plastic "Glamour Girl" In Picnic Day Costume

18" (46 cm). Hard plastic socket-head with Margaret face, blue sleep eyes, real lashes, painted lower lashes, umber tinted eyeshadow, auburn wig in original factory coiffure, five-piece hard plastic walker style body. Near mint condition. MARKS: Madame Alexander (costume). The doll wears "Picnic Day" costume comprising pink polished cotton gown with leaf motif (described in the 1953 Alexander catalog as "green leaves on strawberry pink"), green and black ribbon banding lace lace, yellow sash, muslin hooped petticoat, panties, stockings, black strap shoes, straw bonnet with flowers and black net ties, and hat box with curlers and comb. Model #2001C, circa 1953. $1000/1400

**56. Hard Plastic "Queen Elizabeth" From the Beaux Art Creations**

18" (46 cm). Hard plastic socket-head with Margaret face, blue sleep eyes, real lashes, painted lower lashes, umber tinted eyeshadow, closed mouth with rich red lips, dark blonde hair very elaborate factory-original coiffure, five-piece hard plastic walking body. Excellent condition. MARKS: Madame Alexander (costume). The doll wears "elaborate white brocade court gown and blue Sash of the Garter order" according to her description in the 1953 Alexander catalog, along with long taffeta-lined purple velvet cape with faux-ermine trim, hooped petticoat, panties, stockings, one-strap shoes, fingerless elbow-length gloves, tiara, jewelled earrings and bracelets. Model #2025, Queen Elizabeth from the Beaux Art Creations, 1953. $1100/1500

**57. Hard Plastic Bride With Brunette Hair and Brown Eyes**

15" (38 cm). Hard plastic socket-head, brown sleep eyes, real lashes, painted lower lashes, closed mouth, brunette hair in original factory coiffure, five-piece hard plastic walking style body. Excellent condition. MARKS: Madame Alexander (costume). The bride wears ivory satin gown with long sleeves, lace trim and attached petticoat, lace-edged veil-coronet, panties, stockings, single garter, one strap shoes, and carries bouquet of flowers that match the flowers in her hair. The bride appeared in the Alexander catalog in 1952, available in three sizes. $700/900

**58. Hard Plastic "Story Princess"**
**In Aqua Taffeta Gown**

15" (38 cm). Hard plastic socket-head, blue sleep eyes, real lashes, painted lower lashes, closed mouth, brunette hair in original factory coiffure, five-piece hard plastic walking body. Excellent condition, missing wand. Marks: Madame Alexander (tag). The doll, representing "the gracious and lovely television star of N.B.C. whose program is seen from coast to coast weekly", wears an exact miniature gown of one of the star's gowns, of aqua taffeta with overskirt above the hooped floor-length under skirt, rose petal trim, sequined coronet, aqua panties, stockings, silver shoes. The doll appeared in the 1954 Alexander catalog. $700/900

**59. Hard Plastic Doll in Civil War Costume**
**Of the "Glamour Girls" Series**

18" (46 cm). Hard plastic socket-head with Margaret face, green sleep eyes, real lashes, painted lower lashes, closed mouth, brunette curly wig, five-piece hard plastic walking body. Excellent condition, slight complexion fading. Marks: Alexander (doll) Madame Alexander (costume). The doll wears white taffeta gown with lace trim, magenta sash with roses, decorative roses scattered along the gown, pearls, "beautiful big picture hat of white horsehair braid" (according to 1953 Alexander catalog), hooped petticoat, panties, stockings, shoes. Model #2010B from the Glamour Girls series of 1953. $800/1100

## 60. Hard Plastic "Rosamund" In Yellow Taffeta and Tulle

18" (46 cm). Hard plastic socket-head with Maggie face, large blue sleep eyes, real lashes, painted lower side lashes, umber eyeshadow, closed mouth, auburn hair, five-piece walking body. Excellent condition except torso faded. MARKS: Madame Alexander (costume). The doll wears yellow taffeta ballgown with tulle overskirt and tulle edging, hairband with flowers at each side, yellow taffeta panties, stockings, gold shoes. The doll appeared as Rosamund, described as a bridesmaid, model #1551, in the 1953 Alexander catalog. $600/800

## 61. Hard Plastic Doll in "Royal Evening" of the Beaux Art Creations

18" (46 cm). Hard plastic socket-head with Margaret face, brown sleep eyes, real lashes, painted lower lashes, closed mouth, brunette hair in original factory coiffure, five-piece hard plastic walking style body. Near mint condition. MARKS: Madame Alexander (costume). The doll wears her original costumes, described in the 1953 Alexander catalog as "a gown of chartreuse taffeta trimmed with rosebuds and a big sash of forest green taffeta [that] makes a brilliant and striking combination. Her tiara is gold and set with green brilliants. A truly beautiful creation". With taffeta hooped petticoat and panties, stockings, gold strap shoes, bracelet. Model #2020E named "Royal Evening" from the Beaux Arts series of 1953. $1200/1600

33

**62. Hard Plastic Cissy as
"My Fair Lady" in Ice Capades Costume**
20" (51 cm). Hard plastic socket-head, blue sleep
eyes, real lashes, closed mouth, black sequined skull
cap with exaggerated curls and attached dangle
earrings, seven-piece vinyl adult-shaped body.
Excellent condition, face darkened, one skate blade
missing. MARKS: Alexander. The doll wears official
costume of the 1962-63 Ice Capades depicting "My
Fair Lady", comprising sequined tightly-fitted costume
with overskirt, short jacket, wide sash, very wide
sequined hat with stylized feathers, sequin-trimmed
skates. The costume was created by the costume
designers of Ice Capades for their special-edition
programs; they are one-of-a-kind costumes made to
custom-fit Cissy and in perfect miniature scale of the
life-size costumes. Circa 1962. $1400/1900

**63. Hard Plastic Babs in Skating Costume**
15" (38 cm). Hard plastic socket-head, blue sleep
eyes, real lashes, painted lower lashes, umber
eyeshadow, closed mouth, blushed cheeks, blonde
mohair wig in original factory coiffure, five-piece hard
plastic body. Excellent condition. MARKS: "Babs
Skating" Madame Alexander (costume). The doll
wears her original blue satin skating costume with
gold scalloped edging, marabou feathers at hemline,
sleeves and forming a border on the matching cap,
blue satin purse, flowers at waistband, hair and purse
gold skates. Circa 1950. $500/750

### 64. Hard Plastic Elise
### In Gold Ballerina Costume

16" (40 cm). Hard plastic socket-head, green sleep eyes, real lashes, painted lower lashes, closed mouth, brunette hair in original factory coiffure having short bangs with pageboy curls, seven-piece body. Excellent condition. MARKS: Alexander (doll), "Elise" Madame Alexander (costume). The doll wears her original gold metallic ballerina costume with richly gathered gold flecked skirt, gold sequined trim and head-dress, gold ballet slippers. Circa 1958. $400/500

### 65. Hard Plastic "Cissy" in Yellow Tulle Formal Gown

20" (51 cm). Hard plastic socket-head, blue sleep eyes, real lashes, smoky eyeshadow, painted lower lashes, closed mouth, brunette hair in original elaborate factory coiffure, adult-shaped body. Excellent condition. MARKS: Alexander (doll), Cissy by Madame Alexander (costume). The doll wears original yellow tulle formal gown with frothy layers and floral decorations, taffeta and sheer cotton underslips, taffeta panties, stockings, yellow heeled shoes. Circa 1956. $700/900

**66. Hard Plastic Cissy As "Story Princess"**
18" (46 cm). Hard plastic socket-head, green sleep eyes, real lashes, painted lower lashes, closed mouth with lip color to exactly match her gown, brunette hair in long curls and short bangs, adult-shaped body. Excellent condition. MARKS: Madame Alexander (costume tag), "The Story Princess Doll", Madame Alexander (paper tag on wrist with illustration of the castle where she lived). The doll, representing "the lovely star of N.B.C. television" is described in the 1956 Alexander catalog, wearing deep rose tulle gown with narrow pleats, ruffled neckline, taffeta skirt, pantalets, silver shoes, silver tiara with faux-jewels and carrying a magic wand. Model #1892, 1956 only. $800/1000

**67. Hard Plastic Cissy
From Formal Gowns Series**
20" (51 cm). Hard plastic socket-head, blue sleep eyes, real lashes, painted lower lashes, rosebud-shaped lips, brunette hair in original factory coiffure, adult-modeled body. Excellent condition. MARKS: Alexander (doll), Cissy by Madame Alexander (costume). The doll wears dotted nylon net gown over blush-pink taffeta with side satin sash and garden party hat of horsehair braid trimmed with flowers, with panties, stockings, ankle strap heeled shoes, pearls, large solitaire ring with matching earrings. Model #2160, from "Cissy Models her Formal Gowns" series in 1957 Alexander catalog. $900/1200

**69. Hard Plastic Lissy in Formal Gown**
12" (30 cm). Hard plastic socket-head, blue sleep eyes, real lashes, painted lower lashes, closed mouth, blonde hair arranged in original factory coiffure with short bangs and two coiled buns, hard plastic body with jointed elbows and knees. Excellent condition. MARKS: "Lissy", Madame Alexander New York (costume). The doll wears original pink nylon full-length formal gown with embossed designs of flowers, pink taffeta sash, headband with large shaded roses at each side, net and cotton petticoat and pantalets, socks, one-strap black shoes. Circa 1956. $400/600

**70. Hard Plastic Cissy from The Child's Dream Come True Series**
20" (51 cm). Hard plastic socket-head, green sleep eyes, real lashes, painted lower lashes, rosebud-shaped mouth, brunette hair in factory-original coiffure, adult modeled body. Excellent condition. MARKS: "Cissy", Madame Alexander (costume). The doll wears original white organdy gown with veil lace trim, red satin interwoven ribbon and wide sash, red satin reticule, wide woven bonnet with a border of cotton lace and spray of lilies of the valley, taffeta petticoat, panties, stockings, red strap heels, pearl drop earrings, ring. Circa 1954 model 2095. $700/900

**68. Hard Plastic Cissy As Bride from Fashion Parade**
20" (51 cm). Hard plastic socket-head, blue/green sleep eyes, real lashes, painted lower lashes, closed mouth, blonde hair in original factory coiffure, seven-piece adult-shaped body. Excellent condition. MARKS: Alexander (doll), "Cissy" Madame Alexander (costume tag). The doll wears her original bridal gown with lacy bodice, pink satin sash with pearl circlets, tulle skirt over taffeta underskirt, panties, stockings, silver strap shoes, solitaire ring, pearls, bouquet, and "beautiful Medici cap made of tulle [with] chapel length veil [that] falls gracefully down to envelop her in a misty cloud", according to the description in the 1956 Alexander catalog. Model #2040, 1956. $900/1100

**71. Hard Plastic Cissy**
**As Bridesmaid from Fashion Parade Series**
20" (51 cm). Hard plastic socket-head, green sleep eyes, real lashes, painted lower lashes, closed mouth, blonde hair in original factory coiffure, adult-shaped body. Excellent condition, slight surface dust on arms. MARKS: Alexander (doll), "Cissy" Madame Alexander (cloth tag on costume). The doll wears original gown, described in the 1956 catalog as the color of blue-bells, with metallic threaded bodice and tulle skirt, matching head-dress edged with flowers, blue taffeta underskirt, panties, stockings, silver-heeled shoes, and carries bouquet of blue-bells. Model #2030 from Cissy Fashion Parade series of 1956. $700/900

**72. Hard Plastic Cissy**
**Wearing Lace Blouse and Velvet Pants**
20" (51 cm). Hard plastic socket-head, blue sleep eyes, real lashes, painted lower lashes, blonde hair in original factory coiffure, adult-shaped body. Excellent condition, hair slightly disarray. MARKS: Alexander (doll). The doll wears her original fitted sheer lace blouse with rhinestone buttons, black velvet fitted evening pants, pink taffeta sash with jeweled buckle, black sling-strap heels, pearl drop earrings. Circa 1957, the costume was shown in the 1957 catalog as part of the wardrobe for "the doll who has everything". $400/500

**73. Hard Plastic Elise as Wendy Bride**
15" (38 cm). Hard plastic socket-head, large blue sleep eyes, real lashes, painted lower lashes, closed mouth with richly shaded lips and blushed cheeks, short blonde curly hair in original factory coiffure, seven-piece adult-shaped body. Excellent condition, missing bouquet, pearls and one shoe. MARKS: Mme. Alexander (doll), "Elise" by Madame Alexander (costume). The doll wears her original bridal gown of frothy white tulle with satin bodice, taffeta underdress and sash, tulle veil with Medici cap. Model #1590, in the 1956 catalog. $400/500

**74. Hard Plastic Lissy as Bride**
12" (30 cm). Hard plastic socket-head, dark blue sleep eyes, real lashes, painted lower lashes, brunette hair in original factory coiffure, seven-piece body. Excellent condition. MARKS: "Lissy" by Madame Alexander (costume). The doll wears original bridal gown with lace over taffeta bodice, tulle skirt over taffeta underskirt, satin sash with pearl trim, panties, sling strap shoes, rhinestone trimmed bracelet, veil and head-dress with lace cap, carrying bouquet, with booklet. Model #1147, in 1956 Alexander catalog. $500/700

**75. Hard Plastic Cissette as Queen in Silver Tiara**
10" (25 cm). Hard plastic socket-head, dark sleep eyes, real lashes, closed mouth, blonde hair in original factory coiffure, adult-shaped body. Excellent condition. MARKS: Mme Alexander (doll), "Cissette" Madame Alexander (costume). The doll wears white brocade gown trimmed with jewels, blue-jeweled sash, pearl necklace, earrings, white taffeta underslip and panties, gold sling strap shoes, and silver tiara set with jewels. Model #742 in the 1959 Alexander catalog identified simply as "Cissette dressed as a queen". $400/500

**76. Hard Plastic Lissy in Ballerina Costume**
12" (30 cm). Hard plastic socket head, blue sleep eyes, real lashes, painted lashes, auburn hair in upswept fashion with bangs, five-piece hard plastic body. Excellent condition. MARKS: "Lissy", Madame Alexander. The doll wears original ivory satin tutu with tulle ruffled skirt, pink flowers at waist and hair, peach slippers. Circa 1957. $400/500

**77. Hard Plastic Lissy in Formal Gown**
12" (30 cm). Hard plastic socket-head, dark blue sleep eyes, real lashes, painted lower lashes, auburn hair in original factory coiffure trimmed with flowers, seven-piece body. Excellent condition, shoe straps stretched. MARKS: "Lissy" by Madame Alexander (costume). The doll wears her original gown with lace over taffeta bodice, pink tulle pleated skirt scattered with flowers, pink taffeta underskirt, panties, stockings, silver shoes, pink taffeta sash, with booklet. Circa 1957. $400/500

**78. Hard Plastic Cissette as Ballerina**
10" (25 cm). Hard plastic socket-head, blue sleep eyes, real lashes, painted lower lashes, blonde hair in original factory

coiffure, closed mouth, adult-modeled body. Excellent condition. MARKS: Mme Alexander (doll), "Cissette" Madame Alexander (costume). The doll wears her original gold metallic and tulle ballerina costume, sequin head-dress, gold ballet slippers. Circa 1957. $300/400

**79. Hard Plastic Cissette in Green Velvet Gown**
10" (25 cm). Hard plastic socket-head, blue sleep eyes, real lashes, painted lower lashes, auburn hair in original factory coiffure, adult-shaped body. Excellent condition. MARKS: Mme. Alexander (doll) "Cissette" Madame Alexander (costume). The doll wears emerald green velvet evening gown, faux-fur wrap with a trim of baby roses, taffeta petticoat, panties, black sling shoes. Circa 1958. $400/500

**80. Hard Plastic Cissette in Jacket and Yellow Pants**
10" (25 cm). Hard plastic socket-head, blue sleep eyes, real lashes, painted lower lashes, brunette hair in original factory coiffure, adult-shaped body. Excellent condition. MARKS: Mme. Alexander (doll), "Cissette" Madame Alexander (costume). The doll wears original vividly printed jacket with brass buttons, yellow ribbed pants, sling strap heels. Circa 1958. $300/400

**81. Hard Plastic Cissette in Toreador Pants**
10" (25 cm). Hard plastic socket-head, blue sleep eyes, real lashes, painted lower lashes, blonde hair in original factory coiffure, adult-shaped body. Excellent condition. The doll "attired with great chic" according to the 1957 catalog in which she appeared, wearing long-sleeved lace blouse with rhinestone buttons, black velvet toreador pants, blue sash with pearl clasp, pearls, pearl earrings, black sling heels. Model #905, 1957. $400/500

**82. Hard Plastic "Poor Cinderella"**
15" (38 cm). Hard plastic socket-head, blue sleep eyes, real lashes, painted lower lashes, closed mouth, blonde hair in original factory coiffure, five-piece hard plastic body. Excellent condition. MARKS: Madame Alexander New York (costume). The doll wears her original grey and brown cotton dress with black rick-rack trim and yellow embroidery, yellow cotton apron and bandana, cotton panties, brown shoes, with wooden-handled broom. $800/1100

**83. Hard Plastic "Good Fairy"**
14" (35 cm). Hard plastic socket-head, blue sleep eyes, real lashes, painted lower lashes, closed mouth, blonde mohair wig, five-piece body. Excellent condition. MARKS: Alex (doll), "Good Fairy" Madame Alexander New York (costume). The doll wears original cream taffeta gown with pink underslip, gold metallic trim, wings, crown, stockings, pink shoes, and carries her original jewel-studded wand. Circa 1948. $800/1100

**84. Hard Plastic "Prince Charming"**
15" (38 cm). Hard plastic socket-head, blue sleep eyes, real lashes, painted lower lashes, closed mouth with richly colored lips and cheeks, reddish-caracul wig, five-piece body. Excellent condition. MARKS: Alex (doll), Madame Alexander New York (costume). The doll wears original ivory brocade tunic with attached cape, having gold metallic trim, white tights, gold ribbon garter, shoes, ivory brocade cap with plume. Circa 1950. $800/1100

**85. Hard Plastic "Cinderella" in Ballgown**
15" (38 cm). Hard plastic socket-head, blue sleep eyes, real lashes, painted lower lashes, blonde hair arranged in elaborate original factory coiffure that is held by black snood and decorated with metallic hair ornament, five-piece body. Excellent condition. MARKS: Alex (doll), Madame Alexander New York (costume). The doll wears original blue satin gown with silver trim and stars, taffeta slip and panties, stockings, silver strap shoes. Circa 1950. $800/1100

### 86. Hard Plastic "Fairy Queen"

18" (46 cm). Hard plastic socket-head, blue sleep eyes, real lashes, painted lower lashes, closed mouth, strawberry blonde mohair wig with original factory curls, five-piece body. Excellent condition, few small holes in skirt. Marks: Madame Alexander New York (costume), Fairy Queen, Madame Alexander doll (cloverleaf paper tag on wrist). The doll wears her original ivory tulle gown with metallic braid trimmed bodice, stiffened wings with metallic borders, crown with star, taffeta underskirt and panties, stockings, one-strap shoes. Circa 1950. $800/1100

### 87. Hard Plastic Lissy as "Cinderella"

12" (30 cm). Hard plastic socket-head, blue sleep eyes, real lashes, painted lower lashes, closed mouth with rosy lips and cheeks, blonde hair in original factory coiffure, five-piece body. Excellent condition, slight costume fading. Marks: "Cinderella" by Madame Alexander (costume). The doll wears her original blue satin gown with blue lace ruffles, silver metallic trim, blue taffeta petticoat with tulle ruffle, blue taffeta panties, stockings, silver shoes, rhinestone tiara. Circa 1957. $400/500

### 88. Hard Plastic Cissette as "Sleeping Beauty"

10" (25 cm). Hard plastic socket-head, blue sleep eyes, real lashes, painted lower lashes, closed mouth, blonde hair in original factory coiffure, adult-shaped body. Excellent condition. Marks: Mme. Alexander (doll), Walt Disney's Sleeping Beauty by Madame Alexander (costume). The doll wears original turquoise taffeta gown with gold net overlay on bodice and as veil, gold metallic trim, white taffeta underslip and panties, blue slippers with stars, jeweled tiara, with original labeled box. Circa 1959. $500/700

### 89. Hard Plastic Groom from the Godey Series

14" (35 cm). Hard plastic socket-head with Maggie face, blue sleep eyes, real lashes, painted lower lashes, closed mouth, blonde floss wig styled into muttonchops at the sides, five-piece body. Very good condition, some light costume fading. Marks: Madame Alexander New York (costume). The doll wears original costume of satin shirt with cummerbund, black tuxedo tails jacket, side-stripe pants, black shoes and socks, lapel boutonniere, watch fob. Circa 1950. $800/1100

**90. Hard Plastic "Snow White"**
**With Original Green Paper Tag**
15" (38 cm). Hard plastic socket-head, blue sleep eyes, real lashes, painted lower lashes, umber eyeshadow, closed mouth with ruby lips, black hair in original factory coiffure, five-piece hard plastic body. Excellent condition. MARKS: Walt Disney's Snow White, Madame Alexander (costume). The doll wears her original gold print gown with gold lamé laced-front vest, muslin slip, panties, socks, gold strap shoes, pink hair bow, and has her original green paper hang tag. Circa 1952. $600/900

**91. Hard Plastic "Peter Pan"**
15" (38 cm). Hard plastic socket-head with Maggie face, blue/green sleep eyes, real lashes, painted lower lashes, auburn fleeced wig in tightly cropped fashion, five-piece body. Excellent condition. The doll wears original Peter Pan costume comprising green felt jacket with diamond-point edging, black belt with silver buckle, brown tights, brown felt shoes, green felt cap with red feather. Circa 1953. $800/1000

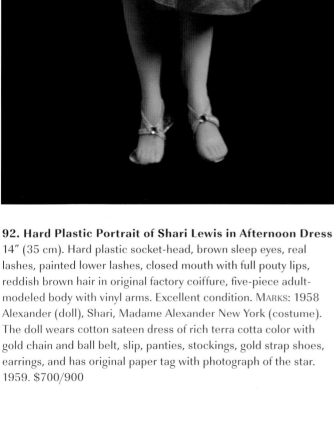

**92. Hard Plastic Portrait of Shari Lewis in Afternoon Dress**
14" (35 cm). Hard plastic socket-head, brown sleep eyes, real lashes, painted lower lashes, closed mouth with full pouty lips, reddish brown hair in original factory coiffure, five-piece adult-modeled body with vinyl arms. Excellent condition. MARKS: 1958 Alexander (doll), Shari, Madame Alexander New York (costume). The doll wears cotton sateen dress of rich terra cotta color with gold chain and ball belt, slip, panties, stockings, gold strap shoes, earrings, and has original paper tag with photograph of the star. 1959. $700/900

**93. Hard Plastic "Mary Martin" In Costume of "South Pacific"**
14" (35 cm). Hard plastic socket-head, brown sleep eyes, real lashes, painted lower lashes, closed mouth, reddish-brown caracul wig, five-piece hard plastic body. Excellent condition. MARKS: Mary Martin of South Pacific, Madame Alexander New York (costume tag). The doll wears original sailor costume embroidered "Mary Martin" on the bodice, socks, shoes, cap, based upon the character role played by Martin in the Broadway performance. Circa 1950. $800/1100

**94. Hard Plastic Portrait of Shari Lewis
In Gold Lace Evening Dress with Original Box**
21" (53 cm). Hard plastic socket-head, brown sleep eyes, real lashes, painted lower lashes, closed mouth with richly shaded lips and cheeks, reddish-brown hair in original factory coiffure, adult modeled body with vinyl arms. Near mint condition. MARKS: Alexander (head), Shari, Madame Alexander New York (costume). The doll wears an "enchanted version of the short evening gown" according to the 1959 Alexander catalog in which she was presented; the unique facial model was used for Shari Lewis doll only. The dress is of gold lace with very full bouffant skirt, pink sash with cascade of roses, imported braid trim, gold necklace and matching bracelet, pearl earrings, emerald ring, yellow taffeta slip, panties, stockings, gold strap heeled shoes, with original box. Model #2430, circa 1959. $900/1200

**95. Hard Plastic Portrait of Shari Lewis
In Gold Lace Evening Dress**
14" (35 cm). Hard plastic socket-head, brown sleep eyes, real lashes, closed mouth, reddish-brown hair in original factory coiffure, five-piece adult-modeled body with vinyl arms. Excellent condition. MARKS: 1958 Alexander (doll) Shari, Madame Alexander New York (costume). The doll wears original gold lame cocktail dress with rose sash trimmed with two little roses, yellow taffeta petticoat, panties, stockings, gold strap shoes, gold pearl necklace with matching bracelet, earrings, solitaire. Model #1440, 1959 catalog. $700/900

**96. Vinyl Elise in Pink Tulle Formal Gown**
17" (43 cm). Vinyl socket-head, large sleep eyes, real lashes, brunette hair in original factory coiffure, coral lips and cheeks, adult-shaped body. Excellent condition. MARKS: Alexander (costume and doll), Elise, Madame Alexander (wrist tag). The doll wears original pink tulle formal gown with ruffles, double petticoats, panties, stockings, shoes, pink bow in hair. 1976. $175/250

**97. Vinyl "Elise" in Pink Ballgown**
17" (43 cm). Vinyl socket-head with large sleep eyes, real lashes, painted lower lashes, coral shaded lips and cheeks, blonde long straight hair and bangs, adult-shaped body. Excellent condition. MARKS: Madame Alexander, New York (costume). The doll wears original pink nylon gown with ruffled neckline and narrow pleats at skirt base, petticoats, panties, stockings, heeled shoes, matching straw bonnet with lace edging, jewelry. Circa 1975. $150/200

**98. Vinyl "Elise" in Rare Yellow Ballerina Costume**
17" (43 cm). Vinyl socket-head with blue sleep eyes, real lashes, painted side and lower lashes, coral shaded lips and cheeks, blonde hair in very elaborate original coiffure trimmed with jeweled tiara. Excellent condition. MARKS: Elise, Madame Alexander (costume). The doll wears her original yellow tulle ballerina costume dotted with rhinestones and little flowers, yellow taffeta bodice and panties, stockings, shoes, black velvet ribbon, earrings, with original box. 1966. $200/300

**99. Hard Plastic Cissy in "Garden Party" Costume in Original Box**
20" (51 cm). Hard plastic socket-head, blue/brown flecked sleep eyes, real lashes, painted lower lashes, closed mouth with richly colored lips and cheeks, blonde hair in original elaborate factory coiffure, adult-modeled body. Near mint condition. MARKS: Alexander (doll), Cissy, Madame Alexander (costume). The doll wears original yellow taffeta dress "with flowers printed all over in profusion" (according to the 1957 catalog description), black satin sash, yellow lace slip, panties, stockings, black strap heels, black straw bonnet with wide brim, watch and fob, cameo, necklace, earrings, bracelet, ring, and original box. Model #2120, 1957. $1100/1500

**100. Hard Plastic Cissy
From Fashion Parade in Black Velvet Gown**
20" (51 cm). Hard plastic socket-head, blue sleep eyes, real lashes, painted lower lashes, rosebud-shaped lips of closed mouth, dark blonde hair in original factory coiffure, adult-modeled female body. Excellent condition. MARKS: Cissy by Madame Alexander (costume). The doll wears original gown described as the "long-stemmed look" in the 1956 Alexander catalog, of black velvet and tulle with a "flared décolletage, lined with pink satin. A cluster of pink rosebuds at the shoulders and deep flounce line are its only trimming. A gown of great elegance." Along with black net petticoat, panties, stockings, bright pink strap shoes, Alexander-labeled hat box, ring, and Fashion Award emblem. Model #2043, 1956.
$900/1300

**101. Hard Plastic Cissette as "Margot"**
10" (25 cm). Hard plastic socket-head, blue sleep eyes, real lashes, sophisticated painting of side lashes and blue eyeshadow, closed mouth, brunette hair in elaborate upward sweep with forehead curl, adult-shaped body. Excellent condition. Marks: Mme. Alexander (doll), "Margot" (costume) Margot by Madame Alexander (wrist tag). The doll wears her original black satin cropped pants, white cutwork cotton tunic, gold sling strap heels, dangle pearl earrings, and has original wrist tag. $500/700

**102. Hard Plastic Cissette in "Tea in the Garden" Costume**
10" (25 cm). Hard plastic socket-head, blue sleep eyes, real lashes, rosy cheeks, brunette hair in bangs and flip curls, adult-shaped body. Excellent condition. Marks: Mme. Alexander (doll), "Cissette", Madame Alexander (costume), Cissette made by Madame Alexander (wrist tag). The doll wears original crisp blue cotton dress with white trim, white taffeta petticoat and panties, stockings, white sling strap heels, white strap bonnet with blue ribbon, pearl earrings, booklet. Model #810, 1958. $550/750

**103. Hard Plastic Cissette as "Jacqueline"**
10" (25 cm). Hard plastic socket-head, blue sleep eyes, real lashes, painted lower lashes, coral lips and rosy cheek blush, dark brunette hair in unique style, adult-shaped body. Excellent condition. Marks: Mme. Alexander (doll), Madame Alexander (costume). The doll wears her original Jackie signature costume of yellow sleeveless sheath under matching yellow linen-like coat with faille lining, yellow tulle hat, panties, stockings, black sling-strap heels, rhinestone earrings and ring. Model #895, circa 1962. $550/750

### 105. Hard Plastic Cissette with Auburn Hair

10" (25 cm). Hard plastic socket-head, blue sleep eyes, real lashes, painted lower lashes, auburn hair with bangs and flip curls, adult-shaped body. Excellent condition. MARKS: Mme. Alexander (doll), Cissette, Madame Alexander (costume). The doll wears vibrant cotton print dress with rhinestone trim at bodice, taffeta petticoat and panties, stockings, orange sling-strap heels, orange straw bonnet with floral trim. Model #707, 1962. $450/550

### 104. Hard Plastic Cissette with Blonde Bouffant Hair

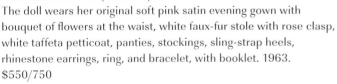

10" (25 cm). Hard plastic socket-head, blue sleep eyes, real lashes, painted lower lashes, blonde bouffant hair, adult-shaped body. Excellent condition. MARKS: Mme. Alexander (doll), Cissette, Madame Alexander (costume). The doll wears her original soft pink satin evening gown with bouquet of flowers at the waist, white faux-fur stole with rose clasp, white taffeta petticoat, panties, stockings, sling-strap heels, rhinestone earrings, ring, and bracelet, with booklet. 1963. $550/750

**106. Hard Plastic Cissette in Costume of Denmark**
10" (25 cm). Hard plastic socket-head, blue sleep eyes, real lashes, painted lower lashes, bright rosy cheeks, blonde hair with bangs and flip curls, adult-shaped body. Excellent condition. MARKS: Mme. Alexander (doll), Madame Alexander (costume), Denmark (gold wrist tag). The doll wears her rare original folklore costume of white organdy blouse, pink taffeta skirt, black vest, mauve apron with metallic edging, lace-edged coif, petticoats, panties, stockings, black sling-strap heels, with original box and wrist tag. One of only two models of Cissette in international costume. Circa 1963. $550/750

**107. Hard Plastic Cissette in Costume of Iceland**
10" (25 cm). Hard plastic socket-head, blue sleep eyes, real lashes, painted lower lashes, dark blonde hair with bangs and flip curls, adult-shaped body. Excellent condition. MARKS: Mme. Alexander (doll), Madame Alexander (costume), Iceland (wrist tag). The doll wears her rare original folklore costume of white organdy blouse with brilliant red taffeta skirt, black apron and vest with metallic and colorful ribbons, embroidered headdress, taffeta petticoat, panties, stockings, red heels, with original wrist tag. Circa 1963. $550/750

### 108. Vinyl Brenda Starr
### In Lace Chemisette

11" (28 cm). Vinyl socket-head, blue sleep eyes, real lashes, pink shaded lips, auburn hair in bouffant style, adult-shaped body. Very good condition. Marks: Alexander 1964 (doll), "Brenda Starr" by Madame Alexander (costume). The doll wears original lace chemisette, and has her original stand and shoes never removed from package, and original box. Model #900, 1964. $200/250

### 109. Vinyl Brenda Starr
### In Lounging Suit

12" (30 cm). Vinyl socket-head, blue sleep eyes, real lashes, pink shaded lips, auburn hair in bouffant and coiled curls at crown, adult-shaped body. Excellent condition. Marks: Alexander 1964 (doll), "Brenda Starr" by Madame Alexander (costume). The doll wears tropical print sleeveless top with sequin trip, hot pink satin long pants, double-strand pearls, heels, earrings, and has additional accessories including gold clutch, two belts, orange bangle bracelet, with box. 1964. $250/300

### 110. Vinyl Brenda Starr
### In Green Print Sheath

12" (30 cm). Vinyl socket-head, blue sleep eyes, real lashes, coral shaded lips, auburn hair in bouffant with upswept braid at the crown, adult-modeled body. Excellent condition. Marks: Alexander 1964 (doll), "Brenda Starr" by Madame Alexander (costume). The doll wears original green print cotton sleeveless dress, panties, pink heels, with original box. Model #905, 1964. $175/250

### 111. Vinyl Brenda Starr
### In Rose Cotton Dress

12" (30 cm). Vinyl socket-head, blue sleep eyes, real lashes, coral shaded lips, auburn bouffant hair style with coiled hair at crown, adult-shaped body. Good condition, some dust on hands and dress, shoes split. Marks: Alexander 1964 (doll), "Brenda Starr" by Madame Alexander (costume). The doll wears original afternoon tea dress of pink cotton with pearl buttons, lace hem, cotton petticoat and panties, white heels, with original booklet and box, and with extra wig. Model #912, 1964. $150/200

### 112. Vinyl Brenda Starr
### In Rose Organza Ball Gown
12" (30 cm). Vinyl socket-head, blue sleep eyes, real lashes, pink shaded lips, auburn hair in short center-parted bouffant with tightly braided coil at top of head, adult-shaped body. Excellent condition, missing shoes. MARKS: Alexander 1964 (doll), "Brenda Starr by Madame Alexander (costume). The doll wears her original sheer rose organza ball gown with very full skirt, embroidered flowers at waist, shoulders and skirt with tiny rhinestone trim, pink organdy petticoat, panties, pearl necklace, with original box. 1964. $250/350

### 113. Vinyl Brenda Starr
### In Emerald Green Evening Skirt
12" (30 cm). Vinyl socket-head, blue sleep eyes, real lashes, coral shaded lips, auburn hair in short center-parted bouffant with coiled arrangement at crown, adult-shaped body. Excellent condition. MARKS: Alexander 1964 (doll), "Brenda Starr" by Madame Alexander (costume). The doll wears her original white lace sleeveless blouse with emerald green taffeta skirt, pink velvet sash with emerald centered buckle, panties, pink heels, pearl earrings, and has her original box. 1964. $250/300

### 114. Vinyl Brenda Starr
### In Gold and Ivory Evening Ensemble
12" (30 cm). Vinyl socket-head, blue sleep eyes, real lashes, coral shaded lips, adult-shaped body. Very good condition, some overall dustiness, shoes not original. MARKS: Alexander 1964 (doll), "Brenda Starr" by Madame Alexander (costume). The doll wears gold metallic sleeveless top, straight ivory satin long skirt with metallic braid and satin overskirt, ivory shoes, with box. 1964. $150/200

### 115. Vinyl Brenda Starr in Bridal Gown
12" (30 cm). Vinyl socket-head, blue sleep eyes, real lashes, painted lower lashes, rich coral lips, auburn hair in bouffant with bridal coronet enclosing a coronet of curls, adult-shaped body. Excellent condition. MARKS: Alexander 1964 (doll), "Brenda Starr" by Madame Alexander (costume). The doll wears multi-tiered white lace wedding gown with satin sash, taffeta petticoat, panties, pearls, earrings, coronet of white flowers and veil, bouquet of flowers. 1964. $250/300

### 116. Hard Plastic "Wendy Ann" in Party Dress
21" (53 cm). Hard plastic socket-head, blue sleep eyes, real lashes, painted lower lashes, smoky eyeshadow, closed mouth with richly shaded lips, light brown human hair with bangs and long curls, five-piece hard plastic body. Excellent condition. MARKS: A.L. (head), "Wendy Ann" by Madame Alexander (costume). The doll wears her original organdy dress with printed dots, lace edging, pink sash with flowers, blue nylon petticoat and panties, white socks, black one strap shoes. Circa 1949. $700/900

### 117. Complete Set of Hard Plastic "Little Women"

14" (35 cm). Each has hard plastic socket-head, blue sleep eyes, hair arranged in very elaborate original factory coiffure, five-piece hard plastic body. Excellent condition, Beth costume a tad dusty. MARKS: Louisa M. Alcott's Little Women (and name of doll), Madame Alexander. Each doll wears original costume, comprising Beth with Maggie face, blue printed skirt with embroidery to suggest apron; Jo with Maggie face, blue checkered dress and red pinafore; Meg with light brown hair, blue flowered dress and cherry sateen pinafore; Amy with blue polka dotted dress and black velvet sash; and Marme with striped cotton dress with black satin apron and black velvet collar and cuffs. Each with original undergarments, shoes and socks. Marme and Amy were shown in these costumes in the 1954 Alexander catalogs, and have walker style bodies. Circa 1954. $1500/1800

### 118. Set, Hard Plastic "Little Women" Dolls with Lissy Face

12" (30 cm). Each has hard plastic socket-head, sleep eyes, real lashes, painted lower lashes, five-piece hard plastic body. Excellent condition. MARKS: Louisa M. Alcott's Little Women (and name of doll, on each costume). Each has original wrist tag, original box, and original detailed costume. 1963. $800/1000

62

### 119. Hard Plastic "Tommy Bangs" From Little Men Series

15" (38 cm). Hard plastic socket-head, green sleep eyes, real lashes, richly painted lips, side-parted blonde hair in boyish style, five-piece hard plastic body. Excellent condition. MARKS: "Tommy Bangs" by Madame Alexander (costume). The doll wears his original green felt jacket with brass buttons, matching cap, shirt, silk tie, twill trousers, shoes, socks, and has Fashion Award paper label on wrist. The doll appeared in the 1952 Alexander catalog. $800/1000

### 120. Hard Plastic "Stuffy" From Little Men Series

15" (38 cm). Hard plastic socket-head with Maggie face, blue sleep eyes, side-parted short boyish hair in dark blonde color, real lashes, painted lower lashes, rosy cheeks, five-piece hard plastic body. Excellent condition. MARKS: "Stuffy" by Madame Alexander, New York. The doll wears his original blue felt jacket and cap, white shirt, black and white checkered trousers, black belt, bow tie and shoes. The model appeared in the 1952 Alexander catalog. $800/1000

### 121. Hard Plastic "Nat" From Little Men Series

15" (38 cm). Hard plastic socket-head with Maggie face, brown sleep eyes, real lashes, painted lower lashes, rosy cheeks, brown side-parted hair in boyish fashion, five-piece hard plastic body. Excellent condition. MARKS: "Nat" by Madame Alexander, New York. The doll wears his original yellow felt jacket and cap, white shirt with red bow-tie, purple twill trousers, brown shoes. The model appeared in the 1952 Alexander catalog. $800/1000

**122. Set, Hard Plastic "Little Women" Dolls with Lissy Face**
Each 12" (30 cm). Each has hard plastic socket-head, sleep eyes, real lashes, painted lower lashes, closed mouth. Near mint condition. MARKS: "Louisa Mae Alcott's Little Women, by Madame Alexander (costume tags on each, with individual name of doll). Included in the model 1225 set are: Beth with brunette hair, pink cotton gown with cutwork pinafore; Amy with blonde hair and polka-dotted aqua dress with organdy apron; Meg with dark blonde hair, lavender and white striped dress with organdy apron and brooch; and Jo with long brunette hair, calico print gown, organdy blouse, red apron; and Marme with brunette hair, green taffeta gown, taffeta apron with black soutache trim. Each doll has complete undergarments, black strap shoes, wrist bracelet and is contained, with beautiful rosy cheeks, in its original labeled #1225 box. Circa 1963. $1000/1300

**123. Hard Plastic Lissy as "Jo" with Jointed Elbows and Knees**
12" (30 cm). Hard plastic socket-head, dark blue sleep eyes, real lashes, painted lower lashes, brunette hair in original factory coiffure with bangs, rarer nine-piece hard plastic body with jointed knees and elbows. Excellent condition. MARKS: Louisa M. Alcott's Little Women "Jo", Madame Alexander. The doll wears her original red cotton sateen gown with black trim, organdy blouse, black velvet neck bow, ruffled petticoat and pantalets. 1958. $300/400

## 124. Hard Plastic Lissy as "Jo"
12" (30 cm). Hard plastic socket-head, dark blue sleep eyes, real lashes, painted lower lashes, brunette hair in original factory coiffure with hair drawn away from face and held in topknot at crown. Excellent condition, shoes and socks not original. MARKS: Louisa M. Alcott's Little Women "Jo", Madame Alexander. The doll wears her original red cotton gown with three rows of trim, organdy blouse, cutwork petticoat and pantalets with red ribbon trim. 1966. $200/300

## 125. Hard Plastic "Marme" from Little Women
12" (30 cm). Hard plastic socket-head, blue sleep eyes, real lashes, brunette hair in original factory coiffure, five-piece hard plastic body. Excellent condition of doll, apron and dress lace have color run. MARKS: Louisa M. Alcott's Little Women by Madame Alexander. The doll wears

her original maroon taffeta gown with white cutwork and embroidered apron, lace-edged cap, undergarments, shoes, socks. 1963. $150/200

## 126. Hard Plastic "Meg" from Little Women
15" (38 cm). Hard plastic socket-head, blue sleep eyes, real lashes, painted lower lashes, rosy cheeks, dark blonde hair in original factory coiffure with forehead bangs, hair drawn away from face into topknot and pageboy curls held by snood, five-piece hard plastic walker style body. Excellent condition. MARKS: Louisa M. Alcott's Little Women "Meg" by Madame Alexander (costume). The doll wears her original white cotton gown printed with blue roses, blue polished cotton apron, white lace-edged collar and cuffs, petticoat, pantalets, shoes and socks. The model appeared in the 1954 Alexander catalog. $400/600

### 127. Set, Wendy Dolls As "Little Women"

Each 8" (20 cm). Each has hard plastic socket-head, sleep eyes, closed mouth, hard plastic body with bendable knees (Jo and Marme with walking style bent knee legs). Good condition, some facial fading, Beth's and Jo's hair a bit disarray. MARKS: Alex (dolls), Alexander-kins (and name of doll, costume). Included are six dolls, Marme, Meg, Jo, Beth, Amy and Laurie each with original tagged costume. Circa 1960. $500/700

### 128. Three Hard Plastic Wendy-kins as "Little Women"

each 8" (20 cm). Each has hard plastic socket-head, bent leg body, sleep eyes, ornately arranged brunette or blonde hair in original factory coiffure, rosy cheeks. Excellent condition. MARKS: Alex (dolls) (name of doll and Madame Alexander, on dolls). The dolls wear original factory costumes. Model #781, Jo, 1965 with box. Model #381, Amy, 1962. Model #781, Jo, 1966, with box. $400/600

### 129. Hard Plastic Cissette Portrette As "Agatha" in Window Box

11" (28 cm). Hard plastic socket-head, dark blue sleep eyes, blue eyeshadow, real lashes, painted side lashes, brunette hair in original factory coiffure, adult-shaped body. Excellent condition. MARKS: Mme. Alexander (doll), "Agatha" (costume). The doll wears her original red velvet gown with lace bodice and cuffs, brooch, tulle and velvet bonnet, petticoat, panties, stockings, black heels, has original "Portrettes" wrist tag and original gold-lid window box with her name. Model #1171, 1968. $400/500

### 130. Hard Plastic Cissette Portrette As "Southern Belle" in Window Box

11" (28 cm). Hard plastic socket-head, dark blue sleep eyes, real lashes, painted side lashes, blue eyeshadow, rosy cheeks and lips, blonde hair in original factory coiffure, adult-shaped body. Excellent condition. MARKS: Mme. Alexander (doll), "Southern Belle" (costume). The doll wears her original white stiffened nylon gown with green ribbon and lace trim, petticoats, panties, stockings, green heels, white nylon bonnet with lavish red roses, has original "Portrettes" wrist tag and original gold-lid window box with her name. Model #1170, 1968. $400/500

### 131. Hard Plastic Cissette Portrette As "Renoir" in Original Window Box

11" (28 cm). Hard plastic socket-head, dark blue sleep eyes, real lashes, painted side lashes, blue eyeshadow, brunette hair in original factory coiffure, adult-shaped body. Excellent condition. MARKS: Mme Alexander (doll), "Renoir" (doll costume). The doll wears original navy blue taffeta gown with pleated ruffle at the hem, stand-up collar, lace trim, red taffeta hat, petticoat, panties, red heeled shoes, has original "Portrettes" wrist tag, original window box. 1968. $400/500

**132. Hard Plastic Cissette Portrette as "Renoir" in Original Box**

11" (28 cm). Hard plastic socket-head, blue sleep eyes, real lashes, painted side lashes, blue eyeshadow, coral shaded lips, rosy cheeks, brunette hair in original factory coiffure, adult-shaped body. Excellent condition. MARKS: Mme. Alexander (doll), "Renoir" (costume). The doll wears original pale blue taffeta gown with pleated hem, lace neckline and cuffs, petticoat, panties, stockings, blue sling-strap heels, blue straw bonnet with flowers, wrist booklet, box. Circa 1970. $400/500

**133. Hard Plastic Cissette Portrette
As "Melinda" in Original Window Box**
11" (28 cm). Hard plastic socket-head, dark blue sleep eyes, painted side lashes, blue eyeshadow, blonde hair in original factory coiffure, adult-shaped body. Excellent condition. MARKS: Mme. Alexander (doll), "Melinda" (costume). The doll wears turquoise taffeta gown with pleated ruffle at hemline, organdy bodice with lace trim, petticoat, panties, stockings, black heels, white strawlike bonnet with cluster of flowers and tulle ties, original "Portrettes" booklet and gold-lidded window box. Circa 1968. $400/500

**134. Hard Plastic Cissette Portrette as "Melinda" in Original Box**
10" (25 cm). Hard plastic socket-head, blue sleep eyes, real lashes, painted side lashes, blue eyeshadow, rosy cheeks, coral lips, blonde hair in original factory coiffure, adult-shaped body. Excellent condition. MARKS: Mme. Alexander (doll) "Melinda". The doll wears her original pink lace multi-tiered gown with ruffled tulle petticoat, panties, stockings, sling-strap heels, pink satin sash with roses, two bows in hair, with original box. Model #1173, 1969. $400/500

**135. Hard Plastic Cissette Portrette as "Godey" in Window Box**
11" (28 cm). Hard plastic socket-head, blue sleep eyes, real lashes, blue eyeshadow, painted side lashes, auburn hair in original factory coiffure, adult-shaped body. Excellent condition. MARKS: Mme. Alexander (doll), "Godey" (costume). The doll wears her original pink taffeta gown with lace overlay, petticoat, panties, stockings, shoes, straw bonnet with tulle and floral trim, has original "Portrettes" wrist tag and original gold-lidded window box. Model #1172, 1968. $400/500

**136. Hard Plastic Cissette Portrette as "Godey"**
11" (28 cm). Hard plastic socket-head, blue sleep eyes, real lashes, painted side lashes, blue eyeshadow, coral shaded lips, rosy cheeks, auburn wig in original coiffure, adult-shaped body. Excellent condition. MARKS: Mme. Alexander (doll), Madame Alexander (costume). The doll wears original yellow taffeta gown with lace overlays, bows, straw bonnet with tulle and flowers, taffeta and tulle petticoat, panties, yellow sling-strap heels, with booklet. 1969. $400/500

**137. Hard Plastic Cissette Portrette as "Scarlett"**
11" (28 cm). Hard plastic socket-head, green sleep eyes, real lashes, painted side lashes, blue eyeshadow, rosy cheeks, brunette hair in original factory coiffure, adult-shaped body. Excellent condition. MARKS: "Scarlett" by Madame Alexander (costume). The doll wears original emerald green taffeta gown with black soutache trim, jacket, matching bonnet with lace trimming at inside brim, taffeta and tulle petticoat, panties, black heels, original "Portrette" booklet, original gold-lidded window box. 1968. $400/500

**138. Hard Plastic Cissette Portrette as "Scarlett"**
11" (28 cm). Hard plastic socket-head, green sleep eyes, real lashes, painted side lashes, rosy cheeks, brunette hair in original factory coiffure, adult-shaped body. Excellent condition. MARKS: "Scarlett" by Madame Alexander (costume). The doll wears a costume that is a near duplicate to #137 except having cameo necklace, no lace at interior bonnet brim, variation of flower, long taffeta pantalets and black sling-strap heels, with original box. Model #1181, 1970. $400/500

**139. Composition "Scarlett O'Hara" With Flower-Print Cotton Gown**

18" (46 cm). Composition socket-head, green sleep eyes, real lashes, painted lower lashes, smoky eyeshadow, feathered brows, closed mouth with ruby lips, dark brunette hair, five-piece composition body. Good condition, light surface crazing, eyes faded. MARKS: Madame Alexander (doll), "Scarlett O'Hara Madame Alexander NY" (costume). The doll wears her original gown with cutwork white bodice interlace with green satin ribbon, rose-patterned green skirt, hooped petticoat, pantaloons with green taffeta ribbon trim, green strap shoes, wide straw bonnet. Circa 1940. $600/800

**140. Hard Plastic "Scarlett" with Cissy Face**

20" (51 cm). Hard plastic socket-head, green sleep eyes, real lashes, painted lower lashes, brunette hair with delicate curls at forehead, adult-shaped body with above-the-knee leg jointing. Very good condition. MARKS: Alexander (head). The doll wears her original white nylon gown with pleated lower skirt, lace-edged collar, green-ribboned trim, nylon petticoat, taffeta petticoat, panties, stockings, rose-trimmed bonnet with green streamers, sheer gloves, locket, ring. Circa 1958, reported to be one in a series of only 12 made during this year and considered extremely rare. $1500/2200

**141. "Scarlett" in Cotton Flowered Gown with Cameo Necklace**
21" (53 cm). Vinyl socket-head with green sleep eyes, real lashes, painted side and lower lashes, blue eyeshadow, closed mouth, long brunette hair, adult-shaped body with above-the-knee leg jointing. Excellent condition. MARKS: Alexander 1961c. (head), "Scarlett" Madame Alexander (costume). The doll wears her original cream cotton gown printed with red and yellow flowers with green leaves and garland trim, organdy ruffle with green silk ribbon and lace trim, straw bonnet with green velvet streamers, green taffeta parasol, ring, cameo necklace. Model #2180, circa 1968. $400/500

**142. "Scarlett" in Red Velvet Gown**
21" (53 cm). Vinyl socket-head with sleep eyes, real lashes, side and lower painted lashes, blue eyeshadow, closed mouth, very dark brunette hair, adult-shaped body with above-the-knee leg jointing. Excellent condition. MARKS: Alexander 1961c. (doll), Madame Alexander (costume). The Scarlett model wears original red velvet gown with lace jabot and sleeves, sunbonnet, stiffened petticoat, panties, stockings, silver strap shoes, with watch and fob, ring, and has her original box. Model #2240, circa 1962. $400/500

**143. "Scarlett" in Green Taffeta Gown**
21" (53 cm). Vinyl socket-head with green sleep eyes, real lashes, painted side and lower lashes, blue eyeshadow, long brunette hair, adult-shaped body with above-the-knee jointing. Near mint condition. MARKS: Alexander 1961 (doll), "Scarlett" by Madame Alexander (costume). The doll wears original brilliant green taffeta gown with jacket and matching bonnet, stiffened petticoat, pantalets with green ribbon trim, stockings, shoes, faux-diamond edged cameo necklace, ring, and has original box. Model #2292, circa 1975. $400/500

**144. "Scarlett" in White Cotton Gown**
21" (53 cm). Vinyl socket-head with green sleep eyes, real lashes, painted side and lower lashes, blue eyeshadow, coral-shaded lips, long brunette hair with green bows, adult-shaped body with above-the-knee jointing. Near mint condition. MARKS: Alexander 1961c. (doll), "Scarlett" by Madame Alexander (costume). The doll wears her original white cotton gown with multi-tiered lace-edged skirt, lace-trimmed bodice, green velvet sash with buckle, stiffened petticoats, pantalets, green heeled shoes, carrying floral bouquet, with pearl-edged emerald brooch and emerald ring, with original box and booklet. Model #2247, circa 1987. $400/500

### 145. "Scarlett" in Ivory Satin Flowered Gown
21" (53 cm). Vinyl socket-head, bright green sleep eyes, real lashes, painted lower lashes, blue eyeshadow, dark brunette long hair, adult-shaped body with above-the-knee leg jointing. Near mint condition. MARKS: Alexander 1961 c. (doll), "Scarlett" by Madame Alexander (costume). The Scarlett model wears original ivory satin gown printed with delicate roses, double lace trim at neckline with green satin ribbons, green velvet sash, wide straw bonnet with roses and green velvet streamers, green taffeta parasol, ring, booklet, and has her original box. Model #2252, circa 1986. $300/400

### 146. "Scarlett" in Ivory Satin Gown with Roses
21" (53 cm). Vinyl socket-head, bright green sleep eyes, real lashes, painted side and lower lashes, long brunette hair, adult-shaped body with above-the-knees jointing. Near mint condition. MARKS: Alexander 1961c. (doll), "Scarlett" by Madame Alexander (costume). The doll wears ivory satin gown printed with multi-shaded large roses, ribbon and lace trimmed collar, green taffeta parasol, wide straw bonnet, green rhinestone necklace, ring, stiffened net petticoat, pantaloons, green strap heel shoes, and has her original box. Model #2210, circa 1976. $400/500

**147. Hard Plastic "Babs" with Rare Skating Outfit**
14" (35 cm). Hard plastic socket-head, blue/green sleep eyes, painted lashes, dark eye shadow, auburn mohair wig, five-piece hard plastic body. Excellent condition. MARKS: Alex (head), "Babs" (costume). The doll wears pink nylon sweater with attached panties and matching stocking cap, burgundy velvet skirt, gold ice skates; a rare version of the skating costume that is usually trimmed with fur. 1949. $1100/1400

**148. Hard Plastic "Binnie Walker"**
**With Faux-Leopard Fur Accessories**
15" (38 cm). Hard plastic socket-head, green sleep eyes, dark eyeshadow, auburn hair in curls with bangs, hard plastic body with bendable knees. Excellent condition. MARKS: Alexander "Binnie Walker" (costume). The doll wears original costume described in the 1955 catalog as "darling bright red taffeta redingote, worn over a simple white dress with red dots, trimmed with venise edging and pearl buttons", along with faux-fur hat and muff. Model #1518, 1955. $600/800

**149. Hard Plastic Lissy in Yellow Organdy Dress**
12" (30 cm). Hard plastic socket-head, blue sleep eyes, blonde hair in short curls and bangs, all hard plastic body jointed at elbows, shoulders, hips and above the knees. Excellent condition, shoe straps stretched. MARKS: "Lissy" (costume). The doll wears original yellow organdy pinafore dress with lace dress, tiny silk flowers, matching bonnet, taffeta petticoat and panties, pink sling strap heels, with booklet. The model was made 1956–1958. $500/600

**150. Hard Plastic "Alice in Wonderland" with Maggie Face**
15" (38 cm). Hard plastic socket-head with blue sleep eyes, upturned nose, blonde hair waved away from face into curls at nape of neck, five-piece hard plastic body. Excellent condition. MARKS: "Alice in Wonderland", Madame Alexander. The doll wears her original blue and white checkered dress with very full skirt, organdy collar and sleeve bands, organdy lace-trimmed pinafore, slip, panties, stockings, black shoes. Model #1874, 1951. $500/700

## 152. Hard Plastic Lissy in Yellow Polished Cotton Dress
12" (30 cm). Hard plastic socket-head, blue sleep eyes, long blonde hair with bangs, waved away from face into ponytail at nape of neck, all hard plastic body jointed at elbows, shoulders, hip and above the knees. Excellent condition. The doll wears yellow polished cotton dress with white organdy apron trimmed with yellow featherstitch, yellow panties, socks, black sandals. The doll has original price label from Gimbels at $8.95. Model #1225, 1956. $400/500

## 153. Hard Plastic "Annabelle" with Maggie Face
18" (46 cm). Hard plastic socket-head, large blue/green sleep eyes, dark blonde hair with bangs and long curls, rosy lips and cheeks, five-piece hard plastic body. Excellent condition. Marks: Kate Smith's Annabelle, Madame Alexander. The doll wears her original white cotton dress with red rick-rack trim, red knit sweater embroidered Annabelle, slip, panties, shoes, socks, red bow in hair. Model #1810, 1952. $600/900

## 154. Hard Plastic Brown-Complexion "Cynthia"
18" (46 cm). Brown-complexioned hard plastic socket-head, amber-brown sleep eyes, black hair with curls at forehead and ponytail, rosy cheeks and richly colored lips, five-piece hard plastic body. Excellent condition. Marks: Madame Alexander (costume). The doll wears white shirt with black bow, plaid pedal pushers, gold chain, socks, black one-strap shoes. "Cynthia", 1952–1953, wearing costume 138T from Alexander fashions catalog. $800/1000

## 151. Hard Plastic "Winnie Walker"
25" (63 cm). Hard plastic socket-head, blue sleep eyes, real lashes, painted lower lashes, umber painted eye shadow, closed mouth with bow-shaped lips, blonde curly hair, five piece hard plastic walker style body. Excellent condition. Marks: "Winnie Walker", Madame Alexander (costume). The doll wears polished pink cotton dress with blue and white patterned sleeves and collar, white rick-rack trim, petticoat, panties, pink felt bonnet, shoes, socks, hat box (empty except for original paper label), brass fashion award symbol. 1953. $600/800

### 155. Hard Plastic Alexander-kins as "Juliet"

8" (20 cm). All hard plastic with straight-leg walker body, blue sleep eyes, blonde hair arranged in elaborate coiffure unique to this model, rosy cheeks. Excellent condition. MARKS: Alex (doll), Alexander-kins (costume), Madame Alexander presents Romeo and Juliet (paper tag). The doll wears magnificent ivory-patterned brocade gown and full coat with red velvet and metallic trim, gilded coronet, panties, gold shoes. Model #473, "Juliet" in the 1955 Alexander catalog was described as "so young and lovely, dressed as shown in the Technicolor production of Romeo and Juliet released through United Artists". $1000/1300

### 156. Hard Plastic Alexander-kins as "Romeo"

8" (20 cm). All hard plastic with straight-leg walker body, blue sleep eyes, brunette flocked hair, rosy cheeks. Excellent condition. MARKS: Alex (doll), Alexander-kins (costume) Madame Alexander Presents Romeo and Juliet (paper tag). The doll wears original purple suit with tights, black felt jacket with elaborate metallic trims, gold boots, purple velvet cap with metallic trims and feathers. Model #474, "Romeo", 1955. $1000/1300

### 157. Hard Plastic Alexander-kins as Golden Ballerina

8" (20 cm). All hard plastic with bent-knee walker body, blue sleep eyes, blonde curly hair with bangs, rosy cheeks. Excellent condition. MARKS: Alex (doll), Alexander-kins (costume). The doll wears gold metallic and net tutu with sequin trim, matching headband, gold slippers. The costume was a match to Cissette and Elise Golden Ballerinas, and was made for one year only, 1959. $400/500

### 158. Hard Plastic Alexander-kins in Pink Ballerina Costume

8" (20 cm). All hard plastic with bent-knee body, blue sleep eyes, brunette hair with forehead bangs, curls at top of head and nape of neck. Excellent condition. MARKS: Alex (doll), Madame Alexander (costume). The doll wears pink satin tutu with pink tulle ruffled skirt, pink tights, peach slippers with pink bows, pink flower in hair. Model #730, "Ballerina", circa 1966. $400/500

**159. Hard Plastic
Alexander-kins as "Baby Clown"**
8" (20 cm). All hard plastic with straight-leg walker body, blue sleep eyes, green painted diamonds around the eyes, red tipped nose, clown decoration at mouth and cheeks, pink flocked hair. Excellent condition. MARKS: Alex (doll), Alexander-kins (costume). The doll wears pink and blue taffeta clown costume with gold braid trim, ruffled collar, green felt cap, silver shoes, and has a little dog. Model #464 in the 1955 Alexander catalog described as "Baby Clown...such a beguiling little fellow in two-tone taffeta suit...his dog's name is Huggy". $800/1000

**160. Hard Plastic Alexander-kins as "Pierrot"**
8" (20 cm). All hard plastic with bent-knee walker body, blue sleep eyes, blonde flocked hair, rosy cheeks. Excellent condition. MARKS: Alex (doll), Alexander-kins (costume). The doll wears pink taffeta clown suit with white pom-poms, pink taffeta hat, peach slippers, has a little giraffe on a gold leash, with original store label from Bullock's for $5.95. Model #561 in the 1956 Alexander catalog that noted he "looks very appealing in his suit and hat of satin". $700/900

**161. Hard Plastic
Alexander-kins "Guardian Angel"**
8" (20 cm). All hard plastic with straight-leg walker body, blue sleep eyes, blonde curly hair with bangs, rosy cheeks. Excellent condition. MARKS: Alex (doll), Guardian Angel (costume). The doll wears ivory taffeta gown with floral trimmed bodice and gold braid trim, petticoat, panties, gold shoes, carries harp, has halo and wings. Model #480 in the 1954 Alexander catalog; in the catalog the doll was named "Baby Angel". $700/900

**162. Hard Plastic Alexander-kins in Scarlett Costume**
8" (20 cm). All hard plastic with bent-knee walker body, blue sleep eyes, blonde hair pulled away from face. Excellent condition. MARKS: Alex (doll), Alexander-kins (costume). The doll wears white organdy gown with red silk ribbons and lace, white straw bonnet with flowers and tulle streamers, silver pearls, brooch, taffeta petticoat and pantalets, red shoes. The dress, representing Scarlett, was sold separately by the Alexander firm and appears on a doll of the same production era. Circa 1959. $400/500

**163. Hard Plastic "Wendy Loves to Waltz"**
8" (20 cm). All hard plastic straight-leg walker body, dark blue eyes, reddish-blonde hair in curls and bangs. Excellent condition. MARKS: Alex (doll), Alexander-kins (costume). The doll wears organdy gown with bands of red rick-rack pleated trim at the collar and hem, ribbon sash, taffeta reticule, red bow in hair, petticoat, pantalets, red shoes. Model #476, the doll appeared in the 1955 Alexander catalog described as "Wendy loves to waltz". $400/500

**164. Hard Plastic "Wendy Goes to Sunday School"**
8" (20 cm). All hard plastic with bent-knee walker body, dark blue sleep eyes, blonde curly hair with bangs, rosy cheeks. Excellent condition. MARKS: Alex (doll), Alexander-kins (costume). The doll wears lavender taffeta dress with lace trim, organdy petticoat and panties, black velvet one-strap shoes, socks, black velvet in hair. The doll appeared in the 1956 Alexander catalog as #587 described as "Wendy goes to Sunday school". $400/500

**165. Hard Plastic Wendy as "Cousin Karen"**
8" (20 cm). All hard plastic with bent-knee walker body, dark blue eyes, short blonde curly hair with bangs, rosy cheeks. Excellent condition. MARKS: Alex (doll). The doll wears long flower-print pique gown with turquoise velvet bodice and rick-rack trim, ruffled petticoat, pantalets, white shoes and socks, white straw bonnet with bluets. The doll has original store label inside skirt, having sold at Bullocks for $6. Model #630, the doll appeared in the 1956 Alexander catalog described as "Cousin Karen who come from the Deep South". $800/1000

**166. Hard Plastic Wendy as "Southern Belle"**
8" (20 cm). All hard plastic with bent-knee body, dark blue eyes, long hair in long curls and bangs, rosy cheeks. Excellent condition. MARKS: Alex (doll), Southern Belle (costume). The doll wears powder blue taffeta gown with lace trim and rose silk ribbons, matching sunbonnet with floral trim, cotton petticoat and pantalets with double row of lace, white stockings, black shoes, and has original paper label. Model #385, circa 1963. $500/700

**167. Hard Plastic Alexander-kins as "Southern Belle"**
8" (20 cm). All hard plastic with bent-knee walker body, dark blue eyes, auburn curly hair with bangs. Excellent condition. MARKS: Alex (doll), Alexander-kins (costume). The doll wears aqua/white striped taffeta gown with lace trim, organdy petticoat and pantalets, white socks, black strap shoes, black straw bonnet with lavish arrangement of berries and flowers. 1956. $500/700

**168. Hard Plastic Wendy as "American Girl"**
8" (20 cm). All hard plastic with bent-knee body, dark blue eyes, long blonde hair in pigtails and bangs. Excellent condition. Marks: Alex (doll), "American Girl" (costume). The doll wears red and white checkered dress with white cutwork pinafore, petticoat, pantalets, white leggings, black shoes, straw bonnet with flowers. Model #388, circa 1962. $400/500

**169. Hard Plastic Alexander-kins as "Alice in Wonderland"**
8" (20 cm). All hard plastic with bent-knee walker body, dark blue eyes, dark blonde hair in curls and bangs. Excellent condition. Marks: Alex (doll), Alexander-kins (costume). The doll wears blue cotton dress with dark blue banding and white rick-rack, white pinafore apron, cutwork cotton petticoat and panties, socks, black one-strap shoes. 1956. $400/500

**170. Hard Plastic Wendy in Americana Costume**
8" (20 cm). All hard plastic with bent-knee walker body, dark blue eyes, blonde hair with curls and bangs. Excellent condition, slight facial fading. Marks: Alex (doll), "Americana" by Madame Alexander (costume). The doll wears plaid pinafore dress with black soutache braid over white blouse, petticoat trimmed with red ribbon and cutwork, pantalets, red stockings, black one-strap shoes, blue straw bonnet with red ribbon. Model #486, listed as Wendy Americana in the 1961 catalog. $400/600

**171. Hard Plastic Alexander-kins as "Davy Crockett"**
8" (20 cm). All hard plastic with straight-leg walking body, blue sleep eyes, auburn flocked hair, rosy cheeks. Excellent condition. MARKS: Alex (doll) "Davy Crockett" (costume). The doll wears suede-like huntsman costume with buckskin fringe, suede belt, "fur" hat, and has long rifle. 1955. $800/1000

**172. Hard Plastic Wendy**
**As "Amanda" in Americana Costume**
8" (20 cm). All hard plastic with bent-knee walker body, auburn hair in two generous curly pigtails at sides of head, rosy cheeks. Excellent condition. MARKS: Alex (doll), "Americana" (costume). The doll wears orange cotton gown with pleated ruffle at hem and sleeves, tiny black braid trim, petticoat, pantalets, blue and white striped stockings, black one strap shoes, black straw bonnet with pink flowers. The doll appeared as Model #489 in the 1961 Alexander catalog described as an old-fashioned girl dressed in ante-bellum costumes. $800/1000

**173. Another Model of Wendy as "Amanda"**
8" (20 cm). A duplicate model to #172, except having whiter complexion and lighter hair. Model #489, 1961. $700/900

**174. Hard Plastic Wendy as "Colonial Girl"**
8" (20 cm). All hard plastic with bent-knee body, blonde hair combed away from face, rosy cheeks. Excellent condition. MARKS: Alex (doll) Madame Alexander (costume). The doll wears polished blue cotton dress with white collar and cuffs, white apron, petticoat, pantalets, stockings, shoes, white cap, and carries tightly woven basket of fruits. The doll appeared in the 1964 Alexander catalog as "Colonial Girl", Model #789. $400/600

**175. Pair, Hard Plastic Wendy "Cow Girl" and "Cow Boy"**
Each 8" (20 cm). Each is all hard plastic with bent-knee body, blue sleep eyes, she with curly blonde hair and bangs, he with brunette flocked hair, both with rosy cheeks. Excellent condition. MARKS: Alex (dolls), "Cow Boy" (or) "Cow Girl" (costumes). The dolls wear Western style costumes of suede-like fabric with fringing, felt flower appliqués, he with bolo tie, both with boots and ten-gallon hats, both with booklets, girl with original price tag of $6.95. Girl, Model #724,1966. Boy, Model #732, 1966. $500/600

**176. Pair, Hard Plastic Wendy "Indian" and "Indian Boy"**
Each 8" (20 cm). Each is all hard plastic with brown complexion, brown sleep eyes, mohair lashes, brunette hair, bent-knee body, rosy cheeks. Excellent condition. MARKS: Alex (dolls), Indian (girl) Indian boy (boy). The dolls wear elaborate Native American costumes with rich beaded and embroidered trim, she with papoose, he with bow. The boy has original booklet, she has original price tag. Models 720 (boy) and 721 (girl), 1966. $500/700

**177. Hard Plastic Wendy "Goes to a Rodeo"**
8" (20 cm). All hard plastic straight-leg walker body, long blonde hair in pigtails and bangs, dark blue eyes. Excellent condition. MARKS: Alex (doll). The doll wears suede-like cowgirl costume with fringe and appliqué felt flowers and leaves, silver edging on jacket, green panties, straw cowgirl hat with upturned brim and matching felt appliqués, white socks, black cowgirl boots with painted stirrup designs. Model #483, described as "Wendy goes to a rodeo" in the 1955 Alexander catalog. $700/900

**178. Hard Plastic Wendy as Hawaiian Girl**
8" (20 cm). All hard plastic bent-leg body, brown complexion, long brunette hair with curls and bangs, dark brown eyes. Excellent condition. MARKS: Alex (doll), Hawaiian (costume). The doll wears original metallic paper "grass" skirt, flower halter, lei with floral decoration and has original booklet. Model #722, 1966. $300/400

**179. Hard Plastic Alexander-kins as Drum Majorette**
8" (20 cm). All hard plastic straight-leg walker body, auburn hair in curls and bangs, dark blue eyes, rosy cheeks. Excellent condition. MARKS: Alex (doll), Alexander-kins (costume). The doll wears elaborate drum majorette costume with green vest over long-sleeved white blouse with attached panties, taffeta full skirt with fuchsia elastic waistband and trim, gold boots, majorette hat with feathers and trim, carrying baton. Model #482 in the 1955 Alexander catalog described as a drum majorette costume for fancy dress parties. $800/1000

**180. Hard Plastic Alexander-kins as "Parlor Maid"**
8" (20 cm). All hard plastic with bent-leg walking style body, dark blue eyes, dark blonde hair in tight curls, rosy cheeks. Excellent condition. MARKS: Alex (doll), Alexander-kins (costume). The doll wears black taffeta dress with white organdy cuffs and apron each trimmed with tatting, lace cap with black velvet ties, embroidered petticoat and panties, shoes and socks, carrying wooden handled duster. Model #579, "Parlor Maid", 1956. 1100/1400

**181. Hard Plastic Alexander-kins as "Priscilla"**
8" (20 cm). All hard plastic with bent-leg walking style body, dark blue eyes, blonde hair waved away from face. Excellent condition. MARKS: Alex (doll), "Priscilla" (costume). The doll wears blue cotton gown with long white collar and cuffs, white cotton apron and cap, petticoat, bloomers, socks, shoes and carries little wicker basket of fruit, with wrist booklet. Model #789, 1965. $400/500

85

### 182. Hard Plastic Wendy-kin with Braids

8" (20 cm). All hard plastic with bent-leg walking style body, dark blue eyes, auburn hair with long braids and bangs. Excellent condition. MARKS: Alex (doll), Wendy-kin (costume). The doll wears red jersey jacket over white top, blue pleated skirt, red bow, petticoats, panties, shoes and socks, red hair bows, paper wrist booklet. 1963, the doll wears a matching costume to the 12" Smarty doll. $400/500

### 183. Hard Plastic Alexander-kin as "Billy Walker"

8" (20cm). All hard plastic with bent-leg walking style body, dark blue eyes, blonde flocked hair in short boyish fashion. Excellent condition. MARKS: Alex (doll), Wendy-kin (costume). The doll wears matching boy's costume to #182 except having blue shorts and different style shoes. The doll appeared in the 1963 catalog as "Billy Walker"; his costume is identical to 12" Artie doll. $400/500

### 184. Hard Plastic Alexander-kin as "Billy"

8" (20 cm). All hard plastic with bent-leg walking style body, dark blue eyes, brunette flocked hair in short boyish fashion, rosy cheeks. Excellent condition. MARKS: Alex (doll), Alexander-kins (costume). The doll wears one-piece suit having white pique shirt above red shorts, little bow tie, red cap, shoes and socks. The doll appeared in the 1959 Alexander catalog as Model #420 "Billy" described as "the boy next door is waiting to join Wendy for an afternoon of fun". $500/700

### 185. Hard Plastic Wendy-kin in "Cotton Dress" with Hair Braid

8" (20 cm). All hard plastic with bent-leg walking style body, dark blue eyes, long blonde curly hair waved away from face into topknot, bangs, and long braid down the back of the head. Excellent condition. MARKS: Alex (doll), Wendy-kins (costume). The doll wears fully lined red cotton dress with white collar, decorated with green braid and tiny white flowers, panties, shoes and socks, black velvet hair bow, has original wrist booklet, and box. Model #622, the doll was listed in 1965 Alexander catalog as "Cotton Dress". $600/800

### 186. Hard Plastic Alexander-kins

8" (20 cm). All hard plastic with bent-leg walking style body, dark blue eyes, short blonde curly hair with bangs. Excellent condition of doll, costume is not original. MARKS: Alex (doll), Vogue Doll (costume). The doll wears Ginny costume of red organdy, red straw bonnet, red plastic shoes. Circa 1960. $200/300

### 187. Hard Plastic Wendy-kin as Basic Doll
8" (20 cm). All hard plastic with bent-leg walking style body, dark blue eyes, auburn curly hair with bangs, rosy cheeks. Excellent condition. MARKS: Alex (back torso), Wendy-kin (costume). The doll wears blue and white checkered panties, shoes and socks, has original wrist booklet and original box with $2 price tag. Model #600, "Basic Wendy", 1964. $400/500

### 188. Hard Plastic Wendy-kin, Model 600
8" (20 cm). All hard plastic with bent-leg walking style body, dark blue eyes, brunette curly hair with bangs, rosy cheeks. Excellent condition. MARKS: Alex (doll), Wendy-kin (costume). The doll wears pink and white checkered panties, socks and shoes, and has original wrist booklet and original box. Model #600d, 1965. $300/400

### 189. Hard Plastic Wendy-kin as Basic Doll
8" (20 cm). All hard plastic with bent-leg walking style body, dark blue eyes, dark blonde short curly hair with bangs, rosy cheeks. Excellent condition. MARKS: Alex (doll), "Wendy-kin" (costume). The doll wears pink lace-edged panties, socks and shoes, has original paper wrist booklet and original box with $2 price tag. Model #300, "Basic Doll", described in the 1962 catalog as "fully jointed, even at the knees and walks or sits very gracefully". $400/500

### 190. Hard Plastic Alexander-kin as "Hansel"
8" (20 cm). All hard plastic with bent-leg walking style body, dark blue eyes, blonde hair in short curls, rosy cheeks. Excellent condition. MARKS: Alex (doll), Alexander-kins (costume). The doll wears white jersey shirt, black suede-like short overalls with blue rick-rack trim, blue and white striped stockings, black shoes. Model #445, "Hansel", 1955. 500/700

### 191. Hard Plastic Alexander-kin in Riding Costume
8" (20 cm). All hard plastic with bent-leg walking style body, dark blue eyes, long blonde curly hair and bangs. Excellent condition. MARKS: Alex (doll), Alexander-kins (costume). The doll wears white short-sleeved shirt, brown corduroy riding pants, brown leather-like belt, brown suede-like boots, brown felt cap, carries crop. Model #571, described in the 1956 Alexander catalog as "Wendy rides well and enjoys cantering around the Park". $500/700

**192. Pair, Hard Plastic Alexander-kins as "Bride" and "Groom"**
8" (20 cm). Each is all hard plastic, she with bent-leg body, long brunette curly hair with bangs, he with bent-leg walking style body and blonde side-parted flocked hair. Excellent condition. MARKS: Alex (dolls), Madame Alexander (bride). The bride wears white nylon and lace gown with long sleeves, petticoat, panties, long matching veil with coronet of flowers, carrying bouquet, with booklet. The groom wears formal velvet jacket with flower in lapel, satin tie with "diamond" stick pin, white shirt, striped pants, black shoes, socks. Bride is model #735, c. 1960. Groom is model #377, circa 1957 described as "handsome in morning clothes" in the Alexander catalog. $500/700

**193. Hard Plastic Alexander-kins as "Queen Elizabeth"**
8" (20 cm). All hard plastic with straight-leg walking body, dark blue sleep eyes, blonde curly hair with bangs, rosy cheeks. Excellent condition. MARKS: Alex (doll), Alexander-kins (costume). The doll wears original white brocade gown with blue banner sash trimmed with faux-jewels, long burgundy velvet cape with white satin lining, silver jeweled crown, bracelet, petticoat, panties, tights, gold shoes. Model #499, the doll was presented in the Alexander 1955 catalog as "Queen Elizabeth" at the time of her coronation. $500/700

**194. Hard Plastic "Wendy Loves to Swim"**
8" (20 cm). All hard plastic with straight-leg walking style body, dark blue sleep eyes, auburn curly hair with bangs, rosy cheeks. Excellent condition. MARKS: Alex (doll), Alexander-kins (costume). The doll wears original lavender swimsuit with lace trim, gold sandals, white sunbonnet , sunglasses. Model #406, 1955. $500/700

### 195. Limited Edition "Easter Girl"

14" (35 cm). Vinyl socket-head, blue sleep eyes, long straight brunette hair with bangs, five-piece rigid vinyl body. Excellent condition. MARKS: c. Alexander 1965 (doll), Madame Alexander (costume). The doll wears pale yellow polished cotton dress with lace bodice and flower, lace bonnet with yellow flowers, organdy petticoat and panties, white tights, beige one-strap shoes, has booklet. 1968, the model was made in a limited edition of 300, only for distribution on the West Coast, the doll has a letter from Frank Martin, the sales representative who commissioned the dolls. $900/1200

### 196. Hard Plastic Wendy as "Easter Girl"

8" (20 cm). All hard plastic with bent-leg walking style body, dark blue sleep eyes, long straight brunette hair with bangs. Excellent condition. MARKS: Alex (doll), Madame Alexander (costume). The doll wears original yellow polished cotton dress with lace bodice, yellow flower, matching lace bonnet with flowers, petticoat, panties, white tights, tan one-strap shoes, has paper booklet "A Doll". 1968, Model #719, the limited edition doll of 200 was made for distribution on the West Coast, especially commissioned by Frank Martin, long-times sales representative for the company in that area. $1100/1400

### 197. Hard Plastic Wendy in Easter Egg, FAO Schwarz Special

8" (20 cm). doll. All hard plastic with bent-leg style body, dark blue eyes, blonde curly hair with bangs, rosy cheeks. Excellent condition. MARKS: Alex (doll) Alexander-kins (costume). The doll wears yellow romper suit with rick-rack trim, stockings, shoes, and is presented in colorful paper mache Easter egg along with four yellow chicks. With original yellow box decorated with lavender flowers, bunnies and Easter eggs, having original FAO Schwarz label. The doll was produced as an exclusive for that New York toy store in 1965. $1500/2000

### 198. Hard Plastic "Wendy Loves Her Ballet Lessons"

8" (20 cm). All hard plastic with straight-leg walking style body, blue eyes, curly brunette hair with bangs, rosy cheeks. Excellent condition. MARKS: Alex (doll) Alexander-kins (costume). The doll wears original white taffeta tutu with white tulle ruffled skirt, leggings, peach shoes with pink bows, coronet with flowers, matching flower at waist. Model #454 in 1955 Alexander catalog, described as "Wendy loves her ballet lessons". $500/600

### 199. Hard Plastic Alexander-kins as "Gretel"

8" (20 cm). All hard plastic with straight-leg walking style body, blue sleep eyes, curly blonde hair with bangs. Excellent condition. MARKS: Alex (doll), Alexander-kins (doll). The doll wears original white blouse, pink taffeta skirt, flowered apron and matching cap, black laced vest, petticoat, pantalets, shoes, socks. Model #470, Gretel, the doll was described in the 1955 catalog as "so charmingly dressed to go walking with her brother Hansel". $400/500

### 200. Hard Plastic Alexander-kins as "Edith the Lonely Doll"

8" (20 cm). All hard plastic with bent-leg walking style body, blue eyes, dark blonde hair with topknot, curls and bangs. Excellent condition. MARKS: Alex (doll), Alexander-kins (costume). The doll wears pink and white checkered dress with rick-rack trim, white apron, petticoat, panties, shoes, socks, pearls. Model #850, 1958, the doll was inspired by the Dare Wright book featured in Life Magazine of that year. $500/700

### 201. Hard Plastic "Maggie Mix-up"

8" (20 cm). All hard plastic with bent-leg walking style body, green sleep eyes, straight auburn hair with bangs, freckles, impish smile, rosy cheeks. Excellent condition. MARKS: Alex (doll), Maggie (costume). The doll wears turquoise and white checkered dress, white apron with matching trim, petticoat, pantalets, white socks,

beige one-strap shoes, has booklet. Model #578, circa 1960, the Alexander catalog of that year described her as having "pixie face and freckled nose". $400/500

## 202. Alexander Cloth Face Musical Doll
10" (25 cm). All cloth doll with mask face having pressed and painted facial features, side-glancing eyes, blonde yarn hair beneath attached white plush bonnet, attached white plush snow suit on box-shaped torso. The doll is attached to a metal stand with music box keywind. When wound, music plays. Included is (not original) lace-decorated wicker cradle. The doll was described in the Alexander catalog as having a "cuddly fabric body" with "hand-painted face" and available in three sizes, 10", 15" and 17". Circa 1952. $500/700

## 203. Latex "Cherub" With Clover Leaf Tag
10" (25 cm). All latex doll with sculpted short brown curly hair, painted facial features, large dark blue eyes, fringed upper lashes, O-shaped mouth, rosy cheeks, vinyl softly padded body. Excellent condition, body a bit discolored, holes in right hand. MARKS: Alexander (doll and costume), Cherub (wrist label). The doll wears white satin angel dress, felt angel wings, halo. Circa 1951. $400/500

## 204. Latex "Farmer" with Original Box
10" (25 cm). All latex doll with sculpted short brown curly hair, painted facial features, large dark blue eyes, fringed upper lashes, o-shaped mouth, rosy cheeks, vinyl softly padded body. Excellent condition. MARKS: Alexander (doll and costume). The doll wears original cotton plaid shirt, yellow pique overalls and matching cap, shoes and socks, and carries little garden tools, with original fashion award box. Model #620B, "Farmer", 1951. $500/700

**205. "Artie" and "Smarty" in Original Carrying Case with Costumes**

Each 12" (30 cm). Each has vinyl socket-head, sleep eyes, closed mouth with smiling expression, five-piece rigid vinyl toddler body, the boy with side-parted rooted red hair, the girl with rooted wispy blonde hair, rosy cheeks. Excellent condition. MARKS: Alexander 1962c (dolls), Madame Alexander (costumes). He wears red jacket, white shirt, blue shorts, white socks, shoes. She wears rose-patterned nylon dress and panties, pink polished cotton hat, basket of posies. The dolls are presented in vinyl carrying case with two pairs of pajamas and two play outfits, brushes and combs, sunglasses and badminton racquets with birdies and balls. The set was an FAO Schwarz exclusive in 1962. $900/1200

**206. Pair, "Smarty" Schoolboy and Schoolgirl**

Each 12" (30 cm). Each has vinyl socket-head, blue sleep eyes, short wispy blonde rooted hair, closed mouth, smiling, five-piece rigid vinyl toddler body. Excellent condition. MARKS: Alexander 1962 (head), "Smarty" (costumes). The dolls wears matching school girl and school boy costumes comprising red jersey sweaters, white cotton shirts, blue pants or pleated skirt, white socks and tan shoes, each with original wrist booklet, boy with original schoolbooks and box, girl with original purse. Model #1155 (girl) and 1150 (boy). 1963. $400/500

**207. Vinyl "Janie" with School Books**

12" (30 cm). Vinyl socket-head, blue sleep eyes, shy smiling expression, blonde rooted hair with topknot, five-piece rigid vinyl toddler body. Excellent condition. MARKS: Alexander 1964c. (doll), "Janie" by Madame Alexander (costume). The doll wears red and white-striped jersey top with attached blue pleated skirt, petticoat, panties, white socks, beige shoes, with original red hairbow, pencil on tassel neck string, arithmetic notebook, wrist booklet. $300/400

**208. Vinyl "Janie" in Red Artist's Smock**

12" (30 cm). Vinyl socket-head, blue sleep eyes, shy smiling expression, blonde rooted hair with topknot, five-piece rigid vinyl toddler body. Excellent condition. MARKS: Alexander 1964c. (doll), "Janie" by Madame Alexander (costume). The doll wears red cotton smock with white Peter Pan collar and cuffs, blue patterned leggings, tan boots, has original wrist booklet. Model #1134, circa 1966. $300/400

**209. Vinyl "Madelaine" with Ball-Jointed Body**
18" (46 cm). Vinyl socket-head, blue sleep eyes, closed mouth, blonde hair in original factory coiffure with curly bangs, hard plastic ball-jointed body, rosy cheeks. Excellent condition. MARKS: Alexander (doll), Madame Alexander (costume). The doll wears original white nylon taffeta dress with tulle sleeves, narrow red piping, matching bonnet with lace trim, petticoat, panties, socks, and red one-strap shoes. Madelaine, 1949-1952. $600/800

**210. Vinyl "Janie" in Party Dress**
12" (30 cm). Vinyl socket-head, blue sleep eyes, closed mouth with shy smile, coral lips, blonde rooted hair with topknot, five-piece rigid vinyl toddler body. Excellent condition. MARKS: Alexander 1964c. (doll), Janie by Madame Alexander (costume). The doll wears organdy part dress with delicately embroidered pastel flowers, with attached petticoat, panties, socks, shoes, with wrist booklet and original box. Model #1156, 1964. $300/400

**211. Vinyl "Janie" in Pink Ballerina Costume**
12" (30 cm). Vinyl socket-head, blue sleep eyes, closed mouth with shy smile on rich coral lips, blonde rooted hair with topknot decorated with pink and white flowers. Excellent condition. MARKS: Alexander 1964 (doll), Janie by Madame Alexander (costume). The doll wears original pink tulle tutu with ruffled neckline, double ruffled skirt, peach shoes with rose ankle straps. Model #1124, 1965. $300/400

**212. Vinyl "Janie" in Tiered Organdy Party Dress**
12" (30 cm). Vinyl socket-head, brown sleep eyes, closed mouth with coral lips, shy smile, long straight brunette rooted hair with bangs and topknot, five-piece rigid vinyl toddler body. Excellent condition. MARKS: Alexander 1964c. (doll), Janie by Madame Alexander (costume). The doll wears white organdy party dress with six rows of ruffled lace edging on the skirt, petticoat, panties, socks, tan shoes, ivory silk hair bow, with wrist booklet. Model #1121, 1965. $300/400

**213. Vinyl "Suzy" in Straw Bonnet and Pinafore**
12" (30 cm). Vinyl socket-head, blue sleep eyes, closed mouth with pink lips, shy smile, long straight brunette rooted hair with bangs and topknot, five-piece rigid vinyl toddler body. Excellent condition. MARKS: Alexander 1964c. (doll), Suzy by Madame Alexander (costume). The doll wears original blue and white-checkered dress with matching bloomers, flowered cotton pinafore, big straw bonnet with checkered band and floral trim, white cotton tights, tan shoes, carrying basket of flowers, with original wrist bag. Model #1150, 1970. $400/500

**214. Vinyl "Janie" in School Dress with Book**
12" (30 cm). Vinyl socket-head, blue sleep eyes, shy smile, coral shaded lips, blonde rooted hair with topknot, five-piece rigid vinyl toddler body. Excellent condition. MARKS: Alexander 1964c. (doll), Janie by Madame Alexander (costume). The doll wears white pique schooldress with red jersey sleeves, red rick-rack on collar, panties, white socks, beige shoes, red hair bow, carries arithmetic notebook and pencil on neck string. Model #1157, circa 1966. $300/400

**215. Vinyl Prototype Boy with Side-Part Blonde Hair**
15" (38 cm). Vinyl socket-head, blonde rooted side-part hair in short boyish style, blue sleep eyes, smiling O-shaped mouth, five-piece rigid vinyl toddler body. Excellent condition. MARKS: Alexander 1961c. (doll). The doll wears handmade blue velvet romper suit with white shirt, knee socks, black shoes. The doll is the Caroline model with original factory-made short boy's hair, and appeared in 1963 as a prototype of John-John; the doll was never marketed. $400/600

**216. Vinyl "Country Cousin" with Patchwork Pattern Dress**
16" (40 cm). Vinyl socket-head with Marybel face, blue sleep eyes, blonde rooted hair with bangs and long pigtails, rigid vinyl body with swivel waist. Very good, costume and face a bit darkened. MARKS: Mme. Alexander 1958 (doll), "Country Cousin" by Madame Alexander (costume). The doll wears colorful dress in patchwork pattern, petticoat, bloomers, socks, black shoes, straw bonnet with flowers, and carries red suitcase with Grand Hotel label. The model was made in 1958 only. $500/600

### 217. Vinyl "Marybel the Doll Who Gets Well" in Presentation Box
16" (40 cm). Vinyl socket-head, brown sleep eyes, closed mouth with coral shaded lips, blonde rooted hair with bangs and long curls, six-piece rigid vinyl body, swivel waist. Very good condition. The doll wears original pink satin costume, pink shoes, and is in original (worn) box with crutches, casts, bandages, and "spots" to designate measles or chicken pox. Model #1670, 1960. $400/500

### 218. Vinyl "Kelly" with Pink Pinafore
16" (40 cm). Vinyl socket-head, blue sleep eyes, O-shaped closed mouth, dark blonde rooted hair with bangs and long curls, pierced ears, rigid vinyl toddler body with swivel waist. Very good condition, spotting on sleeves, earrings and pearls may not be original. MARKS: Mme. Alexander 1958 (doll). The doll wears blue and white-checkered dress with matching bloomers, pinafore with rick-rack trim, flowers in pocket, earrings, socks, black shoes. Model #1602, "Kelly", circa 1959.

### 219. Vinyl "Mimi" in Capri Costume
30" (76 cm). Vinyl socket-head portraying older child, blue "flirty" eyes, mohair lashes, short brunette rooted hair, pierced ears, shapely torso with swivel waist, arms modeled bent at elbows, swivel wrists and ankles. Excellent condition, some color run on blouse. MARKS: Alexander 19c.61 (doll), "Mimi" by Madame Alexander (costume). The doll wears original pink, green and white striped jersey, turquoise capri pants, black sandals, blue straw hat with flowers, bell-shaped earrings and charm bracelet, with original store label and price of $18.95. Model #3010, 1961. $600/800

### 220. Vinyl "Little Shaver" with Telephone

12" (30 cm). Vinyl socket-head, blue painted side-glancing eyes, brunette rooted hair in wispy fashion, vinyl five-piece baby body. Excellent condition. MARKS: Mme. Alexander (doll), "Little Shaver" created by Madame Alexander (wrist booklet). The doll wears pink cotton panties with lace ruffles, pearls, and owns a pink telephone, with original wrist booklet and box. Model #2950, 1963-1965. $300/400

### 221. Vinyl "Little Butch" with Original Box

9" (23 cm). Vinyl socket-head, blue sleep eyes, hole in mouth for bottle, short blonde rooted baby hair, five-piece vinyl baby body. Excellent condition. MARKS: Alexander 1965c. (doll), "Little Butch" by Madame Alexander (costume). The doll wears white jersey shirt with blue collar, blue pique shorts with straps, socks, shoes, and owns a pacifier and baby bottle. With original paper detailing the doll: it can be bathed, drink its bottle, wet its diaper, cry real tears, and go to sleep. With original box. Model #2720, 1967–1968. $150/200

### 222. Vinyl "Little Shaver" with Original Box

12" (30 cm). Vinyl socket-head, painted blue side-glancing eyes with large black pupils, chubby cheeks, short brunette rooted hair in wispy fashion, five-piece vinyl baby body. Excellent condition. MARKS: Mme. Alexander (doll), Little Shaver by Madame Alexander (costume). The doll wears blue and white-striped jersey sweater, pink bloomers, pink hair bow, has original wrist booklet and original box. Model #2933. 1963–1965. $300/400

### 223. Vinyl "Binnie" with Strawberry Pinafore

18" (46 cm). Vinyl socket-head, blue sleep eyes, chubby face, rosy cheeks, brunette rooted curly hair and bangs, five-piece rigid vinyl toddler body. Excellent condition. MARKS: Alexander 1964c. (doll), Madame Alexander (costume). The doll wears white pique dress with strawberry applique, red jersey sleeves and red rick-rack collar, matching bonnet with rick-rack edging, bloomers, socks, red shoes, carries little lace edged purse with strawberry applique and gold-plated pocket watch and brooch. With original wrist booklet and box. Model #1830, "Binnie", 1964. $400/500

**224. Vinyl "Polly" in Red Velvet Suit**
17" (43 cm). Vinyl socket-head, large blue sleep eyes, O-shaped mouth, blonde hair with upswept hair and bangs tied with red velvet bow, pierced ears, hard plastic body with vinyl arms, high heel feet, legs jointed at hips and ankles. Excellent condition, few spots on skirt. MARKS: Mme. Alexander (doll), "Polly" by Madame Alexander (costume). The doll wears red velvet jacket and skirt, nylon taffeta blouse with lace ruffles, panties, pearl necklace and earrings, bracelet, with booklet. Model #1731, 1965. $350/450

**225. Vinyl "Mary Ellen", Exclusive for Marshall Fields**
17" (43 cm). Vinyl socket-head, blue sleep eyes, closed mouth with slight smile, long blonde rooted hair with bangs and black hair bow, five-piece vinyl body. Excellent condition. MARKS: Alexander Doll 1965 (doll), Madame Alexander (costume). The doll wears blue cotton polka-dot dress with aqua and cream striped sash and ruffle, matching shoes, petticoat, panties, stockings. Model #1715, "Mary Ellen" with Polly face, made exclusively for Marshall Fields in 1965. $500/600

**225A. Accessory Set for Binnie Walker**
Comprising white faux-fur mittens, hat muff and collar, each with white nylon taffeta lining, in original box. Model #428 in 1956 Alexander catalog that described the set as "orlon ermine lined with white taffeta". Excellent condition. $200/250

**226. Vinyl "That Girl" with Mod Costume**
17" (43 cm). Vinyl socket-head, brown glass sleep eyes, closed mouth, long brunette rooted hair with flip curls and bangs, five-piece vinyl body. Excellent condition. MARKS: Alexander 1966 (doll), "That Girl" (costume). The doll wears blue and green jersey knit dress with lining, slip, panties, net stockings, tall boots, pearls, green bow in hair, with original box. Model #1789, based upon the character of Marlo Thomas in the television series "That Girl", 1967. $400/500

**227. Vinyl "Polly" in Lace Dress**
17" (43 cm). Vinyl socket-head, green sleep eyes, closed mouth with hint of smile, long blonde rooted hair with bangs and attached chignon, five-piece vinyl body. Excellent condition. MARKS: Alexander Doll Co, Inc. (1965) Madame Alexander (dress). The doll wears lace dress over blue lining, blue taffeta slip and panties, stockings, grey heels, ivory hair bow. Model #1724, 1965. $300/350

**228. Vinyl "Mary Ellen Playmate",
Exclusive for Marshall Fields**
17" (43 cm). Vinyl socket-head, green sleep eyes, closed mouth with hint of smile, long brunette rooted hair with flip curls and bangs, five-piece vinyl body. Very good condition, missing ring,

shoes. MARKS: Alexander Doll 1965 (doll), Madame Alexander (costume). The doll wears pale pink organdy gown with tiered lace trim and collar, taffeta petticoat with tulle edging, panties, stockings, flowers in hair. The Mary Ellen Playmate, with Polly face, was exclusively made for Marshall Fields, 1965. $300/400

**229. Vinyl "Polly Ballerina"**
17" (43 cm). Vinyl socket-head, brown sleep eyes, closed mouth with hint of smile, light brown rooted hair, rosy cheeks, five-piece vinyl body. Very good condition, holes in stockings. MARKS: Alexander Doll (doll), "Polly" (costume). The doll wears turquoise ballerina costume with sequined bodice, tulle pleated skirt, stockings, shoes, flowers in hair. Model #1725, 1965. $300/400

**230. Vinyl "Polly" in Orange Dress**
17" (43 cm). Vinyl socket-head, blue sleep eyes, closed mouth with hint of smile, brunette rooted hair, five-piece vinyl body. Excellent condition. MARKS: Alexander Doll (doll), "Polly" (costume). The doll wears orange cotton dress with contrasting polka-dot ruffled petticoat with stiffened tulle edging, panties, stockings, orange shoes, orange hair bow. Model #1715, 1965. $300/400

**231. Vinyl "That Girl" in Mod Costume**
17" (43 cm). Vinyl socket-head, brown sleep eyes, closed mouth, long brunette rooted hair with flip curls and bangs, five-piece vinyl body. Excellent condition. MARKS: Alexander 1966 (doll), "That Girl" (costume). The doll wears blue and green jersey mini dress with full lining, slip, panties, fishnet stockings, tall boots, pearls, green hair bow. Model #1789, "That Girl", 1967. $300/400

**232. Vinyl "Maggie" with Green Jacket**
17" (43 cm). Vinyl socket-head, large green sleep eyes, long curly lashes, reddish brown rooted hair in long straight fashion with bangs, five-piece rigid vinyl body with slender torso and limbs, rosy cheeks. Excellent condition. MARKS: Alexander 1968 (doll), "Maggie" by Madame Alexander (costume). The doll wears green felt jacket with double-breasted brass buttons over long-sleeved white blouse, plaid pleated skirt, petticoat, panties, stockings, black heeled shoes with brass buckles, widely brimmed straw bonnet with green grosgrain band. With original wrist booklet and original box. Model #1720, "Maggie", 1972. $250/350

**233. Complete Large Set of Dolls from "Sound of Music"**
11"–17" (28-43cm). The set comprises seven dolls: 11" Marta, Gretl and Friedrich; 14" Louisa, Leslie and Brigitta; and 17" Maria, with a variety of faces and hair styles, each wearing their original costume as represented in the popular musical. The set was made 1966-1970. Excellent condition. $1100/1300

### 234. Portrait "Coco" Model as Scarlett

20" (50 cm). Vinyl socket-head with unique sculpting of head and body only for Coco dolls, almond-shaped brown sleep eyes, real lashes, prominent side-painted lashes, painted lower lashes, closed mouth, long brunette hair, adult-shaped body with swivel waist, model-shaped and posed legs. Excellent condition. MARKS: Alexander (head) Madame Alexander (costume). The doll, presented as "Scarlett", wears her original white tulle gown with lace bodice and skirt border, pearl-edged neckline, rose trim, red sash, white bonnet with white flowers, two petticoats, panties, stockings, red-bowed shoes. 1966, made for one year only. $900/1200

### 235. Portrait "Coco" Model as Godey

20" (20 cm). Vinyl socket-head with unique sculpting of head and body only for Coco dolls, almond-shaped blue sleep eyes, real lashes, painted side lashes and lower lashes, blonde hair, adult-shaped body with swivel waist, model-shaped and posed legs.

Excellent condition, slight fading of skirt front. MARKS: Alexander (head) Madame Alexander (costume). The doll, presented as "Godey", wears original red taffeta gown with black velvet jacket, black tulle bonnet with roses, petticoats, panties, stockings, red shoes, ring. 1966, made for one year only. $900/1200

### 236. Portrait "Coco" Model as Melanie

20" (50 cm). Vinyl socket-head with unique sculpting of both head and body only for Coco, blue sleep eyes, real lashes, prominently painted side lashes, painted lower lashes, blonde hair with coiled braids and curls, adult-shaped body with swivel waist, model-shaped and posed legs. Excellent condition. MARKS: Alexander (head) Madame Alexander (costume). The doll, presented as "Melanie", wears her original aqua taffeta gown with lace and pleats, petticoats, panties, stockings, (one) silver shoe, flowers in hair, cameo necklace, ring. 1966, made for one year only. $900/1200